Getting a Church Started

A student manual for the theological foundation and practical techniques of planting a church.

by Elmer Towns

© 1985
Church Growth Institute
P.O. Box 4404, Lynchburg, VA 24502

TABLE OF CONTENTS

Chapter 1. Introduction **5**
Beginning a church is not an automatic task even when the principles of this book are followed. Planting a church is an insurmountable task, but it can be accomplished. It faces difficult circumstances, but can be victorious. It usually is conceived with limited resources, but history demonstrates that churches will prosper because this task is the genius of Christianity.

SECTION I. BIBLICAL FOUNDATION FOR CHURCH PLANTING

Chapter 2. The Biblical Basis of Church Planting. **11**
Church planting is the logical outcome of the Great Commission and the best method to evangelize the exploding population centers of America.

Chapter 3. Church Planting and the Nature of a Church **21**
The church planter must understand the Biblical nature of the church that he is starting. Many new congregations have failed because they did not fit the New Testament criteria of a church.

Chapter 4. The Role of the Church Planter **29**
The church planter must understand his gift, calling and office to successfully bring a New Testament church into existence.

Chapter 5. The Theology of the Chartering Service **45**
The chartering service recognizes that a new congregation has been brought together by God and that it is now recognized as a New Testament church that can administer the ordinances.

Chapter 6. Biblical Answers to Questions About Church Planting. . **55**
There are many questions a church planter must answer according to the Word of God if he will have the full blessing of God on the new church.

SECTION II. SIX METHODS OF CHURCH PLANTING

Chapter 7. Mother-Daughter Church Planting. **69**
Many churches have been successfully mothered by a mature congregation to evangelize a new area.

Chapter 8. Mission Sunday School Church Planting. **75**
Many mission Sunday Schools never become a New Testament church, but other missions grow in outreach and nurture so that they become an indigenous church.

Chapter 9.   Bible Study Church Planting. **85**
Bible study groups have been used of God to reach many individuals for Christ. However, those that become a church apply principles that are contained in this chapter.

Chapter 10. Associational Efforts to Plant a Church. **91**
Some new churches are the result of the cooperative efforts of a group of churches. Whereas no one may be strong enough to plant a church by itself, several can fellowship together for the task.

Chapter 11. Planting a Church From a Church Split. **97**
There are many tragedies involved in a church split, and in some occurrences a new congregation emerges out of the turmoil. If certain biblical principles are followed, a New Testament church can emerge out of the ashes of a church split.

Chapter 12. The Pioneering Church Planter **105**
The pioneering church planter does not work through a mothering church, mission Sunday School or Bible study class. He goes to an area because God has called him there to start a new church to evangelize the area for Christ.

SECTION III.   84 STEPS TO PLANT A CHURCH

Chapter 13. Steps to Plant a Church **117**
There is no one correct avenue in starting a church, but there are general guidelines that the church planter should follow if he wants to be successful.

SECTION IV.   APPENDIX

Chapter 14. Constitution **167**
Many soul winning churches fail because they have used the traditional church constitution that gave the leadership of the church to someone other than the pastor or organized the church for purposes other than fulfilling the Great Commission.

Chapter 15. Chartering Statement **177**
This statement has been used to charter new churches for almost 200 years. It places the burden upon "We the people" so that congregational autonomy is both the foundation and continuation of the new church.

Chapter 16. Community Survey **179**
When the church planter has a knowledge of the area where he is going, God is able to give him clearer leading and the church will grow more healthy because

it will probably have to overcome fewer problems in its future.

Chapter 17. Liberty Baptist Fellowship for Church Planting. . . . **185**
Liberty Baptist Fellowship for Church Planting is the organizational arm of Liberty Baptist Schools to plant 5,000 new churches by 2000 A.D. The material in this section explains the nature of a fellowship of Baptist churches to plant new churches.

Model News Release **189**

For Further Study **191**

Directory **192**

CHAPTER 1

INTRODUCTION

Starting a church is exciting, but never an easy task. The miracle of birth is just as evident in church-planting as when a child is born. The world is not hospitable to soul-winning. Most new churches begin with inadequate facilities and limited resources. It almost seems that if they are too financially prosperous, their vitality is not. Like pioneering families, the greatest victories are won only against the most threatening foes. There is no ideal place to start a church. The Bible Belt is not ideal because people are gospel-hardened and areas are over-churched. The Catholic neighborhood has a built-in religion barrier; and cold northern cities reject soul-winning churches, calling them religious fanatics. New churches are always conceived in the heart of their founder and born in adversity. New churches challenge us to "think the impossible" and "expect the victorious." God still uses those who step out on faith, follow his plan and tenaciously agonize in work.

Starting new churches is the genius of Christianity. As the population explodes and another community comes into existence, new churches are needed. As old churches lose their fervency and slip into liberalism, new churches are needed to take their place.

Wendell Belew of the Southern Baptist Home Mission Board plans over 500 new churches in America every year. Someone asks, "What method do you plan to use to plant 500 new churches a year?" He replies, "For 500 churches, we need 500 methods."

Every community has different needs and every group of people reflects a different composite personality. Each pastor must minister according to his spiritual gifts, hence there is a different application of Biblical principles in every new church.

New churches are successful in rural, small towns, city and metropolitan areas. Men use a different formula in building each church. Yet, many patterns are similar because certain timeless principles transcend space and culture. These grow out of the nature of the church and the principles in the New Testament.

Some churches have grown faster than others. No church is perfect - like young children they are growing through the pains of childhood. But even in youth, there is something compelling about a child. Each church, as reflected in each of its pastor-founders, has different strengths, hence each is a different example to guide those building a church.

I don't consider myself an authority on establishing new churches. I have interviewed men and have written their stories. They are the authorities; I am simply the channel through which the story is written. My interest in church-founding came after realizing that four of the churches in the book *The Ten Largest Sunday Schools* were begun by the present pastor. Also, I wrote a series on great soul-winning churches in *The Sword of the Lord*. A great number of these also were started by the present pastor. The idea for this book came in the spring, 1973, when as Academic Dean of Lynchburg Baptist College, I arranged for a chapel series on *How To Start A Church*, and invited eight pastors to share with the student body the lessons they learned.

While a student at Columbia Bible College, South Carolina, I re-organized and pastored the Westminster Presbyterian Church, Savannah, Georgia, (1951-53) - a church building with property but the congregation had gone out of existence. While at Dallas Theological Seminary, I organized and pastored Faith Bible Church (1956-58). It had previously been a Sunday School mission.

Some will not be able to follow the principles of this book and start a successful church because they have different concepts about the church. The end product always determines the process. The end product in this book is a soul-winning, Bible-teaching church that stands for purity, obedience to the Great Commission, and separation from apostasy. Therefore, if this is not the type of church a man wants to build, all of these principles will not apply to his situation. But, in fact, not all of these principles will apply in any situation. They must be read in light of Scripture, applied in relationship to the community, and integrated by the man of God.

The church is close to the heart of God (Eph. 5:25) and those who start a church have a special place in God's affection. When preaching on the doctrine of the church, I often ask for charter members of that congregation to raise their hands. These, I note, have a special place in God's love for the sacrifice, vision, and labor that brought a church into existence. One of the greatest privileges in life is to help bring a candlestick (Rev. 2:1,5) into existence.

Appreciation is expressed to Mr. Doug Porter who worked as Research Assistant on this project. Not only was he invaluable in research, his commitment to church planting was reassuring. After graduation from Liberty Baptist Seminary, Mr. Porter plans to return home to Oakville, Ontario, Canada and plant the Oakland Heights Baptist Church.

May God use this manuscript according to its potential.

                        ELMER TOWNS

                        Lynchburg, Virginia

Winter 1982

SECTION I

BIBLICAL FOUNDATION FOR CHURCH PLANTING

Too often church planting is considered only in terms of techniques. This limited view thinks only of getting the church planter at a needy place with the right techniques, with enough money and a church will evolve. There is a spiritual and theological side to church planting. The man of God must properly apply the Great Commission (Chapter 2) which involves soul winning and church planting. Next, the man of God must understand the biblical nature of the church, or he will fail in his efforts to plant one (Chapter 3). The man of God must understand his calling from God, his spiritual gifts and the church office he assumes (Chapter 4). Next, the church planter must understand the theological steps necessary to lead a group of people to become a New Testament church (Chapter 5). Finally, this section answers the following questions, "Who can begin a church?", "Should a man begin a church in his boyhood home?", "Shall a new church be named Baptist?", and "How shall finances be given to a new church?" These questions have practical answers but the correct answer is rooted in New Testament theology.

CHAPTER 2

THE BIBLICAL BASIS OF CHURCH PLANTING

No one questions the command of the Great Commission to go and win lost people to Jesus Christ. But Independent Baptists believe that the second aspect of the Great Commission is planting New Testament churches, for this is the means to reach lost people in every culture of the world. In a simplistic observation, one of the reasons why so much foreign missions is fruitless, is because great effort is spent on winning people apart from a New Testament church. All evangelism has its place; radio evangelism, television evangelism, medical evangelism, mass evangelism, personal evangelism, educational evangelism, humanitarian evangelism. But God's primary method of evangelizing an area is by planting a New Testament church to reach the area with the gospel.

But some are ignorant of this method, while others disagree. They deny that church planting is in the Great Commission. A careful study of the Great Commission will reveal the complex and divergent nature under which it was given, but also the student will see the different task that Jesus wanted accomplished.

In Matthew 28:19 the command includes discipling "all the nations" or peoples. Mark 16:15 includes the entire world as the sphere and every creature (person) as the goal to which the gospel is to be proclaimed. Luke 24:47,48, directs us that the message of Christ's offer of forgiveness for sins is to be taken into all the nations beginning from Jerusalem. John 20:21 promises spiritual power to those who are sent. Acts 1:8 teaches that when filled with the Holy Spirit, believers are to witness of the facts of salvation to the most remote, farthest point of the earth.

The Great Commission was given at five different times in separate locations. On each occasion the Lord added to the previous command and the reader must see the total picture to understand the full implication of the Great Commission.

	WHERE	WHEN	TO WHOM	WHAT	KEY
1. John 20:21	Upper room Jerusalem	Resurrection	10 disciples	I am sending you	Commission
2. Mark 16:15	Upper room Jerusalem	One week later	11 disciples	Go to all the world & preach to every person	Recipient
3. Matt. 28: 19, 20	Mountain in Galilee	At least two weeks	11 disciples	Disciple all "peoples" then baptize & teach	Strategy
4. Luke 24: 46-48	Jerusalem	40th day	11 disciples	Preach repentance & forgiveness of sins based on resurrection of Christ	Content
5. Acts 1:8	Mt. of Olive	40th day	11 disciples	Jerusalem to uttermost part of earth	Geography

Notes

Note the third giving of the Great Commission in Matt. 28 includes strategy. The first aspect is to go to every person and evangelize them individually. The second aspect implies to evangelize all peoples through planting churches where people can be baptized and continually be discipled and taught the Word of God. It is with this in mind that Virgil Gerber concludes that "the ultimate evangelistic goal in the New Testament, therefore, is twofold: (1) to make responsible, reproducing Christians, (and) (2) responsible, reproducing congregations.

The Great Commission in Matthew includes church planting.

1. Because the command "to disciple" Μαθητεύσατε includes the beginning and the continuing ministry of discipling people. This was fulfilled in the church in the New Testament.

2. Because the command "to baptize" is a participle, meaning they were to keep on baptizing. Since this was carried out by churches in the New Testament, and baptism identifies a person with the church, then the result of evangelizing a new area ἔθνη was to plant a church so new believers could be baptized into it.

3. Because the command, "teaching them to observe" is carried out in the New Testament church by "teaching the apostles doctrine: (Acts 2:49) which was the basis of their growth and fellowship; therefore when new areas are evangelized, there must be new churches where new believers are taught these things.

4. Because by illustration the New Testament churches went everywhere establishing churches. Wherever the gospel was successful, a church sprung into existence.

5. Because by analogy each produces after its kind, a church that sends out a missionary who should plant churches that also send out missionaries.

Beginning with the great dispersion of the Jerusalem believers recorded in Acts 8, the disciples successfully multiplied congregations and planted additional churches. In fact "new congregations were planted in every pagan center of the then-known world in less than four decades."[2] As the believers were scattered, so was the seed of the gospel that would take root in various national soils. In Acts 9:31 a geographical broadening takes place so that believers are placed (as directed in Acts 1:8) "throughout all Judea and Galilee and Samaria" (NASB). Based on the understanding of the eleven disciples and the success that resulted from their obedience, it is evident that planting local churches in every city throughout the world is God's plan.

The dynamic church-planting efforts of the Apostle Paul, Barnabas and Silas, Timothy, and others who were all early disciples verifies the concept of local church expansion to which Jesus Christ is committed. Surely they would have done no less than He commanded and no more than He empowered.

High on the list of practical issues that face the growing church today is the commitment and planning that are necessary to begin other works. Costas agrees that:

> Another principle of church growth strategy is the concentration on congregational multiplication in established church situations rather than in increasing the membership role of one local congregation. Wagner says that "the best way for a church to grow . . . is to be active in reproducing itself." He warns that such an enterprise is bound to be costly. It will cost people, time, money, and identification, but the fruit it will produce will make the sacrifice

Notes

worth while.³

Concerning church multiplication in Thailand, Paul Davis, one of 800 missionaries of the Christian Missionary Alliance Church, writes:

> From the day God said to Adam and Eve, "Be fruitful, multiply, replenish the earth," multiplication has been the secret of the growth of the human race, until this geometric progression has reached the staggering proportions of a population explosion.
>
> Christians will lose the race to tell the world of Christ unless we are converted from our dedication to mere addition which slowly increases an organization, and begin diligently to apply to the living Church the principle of multiplication, so characteristic of the growth of a living organism.
>
> Our experience in Thailand seems to indicate two dangers: (1) we aim too low--individual; (2) we aim too high--the district organization, the national organization.
>
> Even when we grasp the simple fact that multiplication is the secret of the growth of the church, we need to ask--a multiplication of what? Not committees, not high offices, not even individual believers as such. We must apply our secret at the level of the local church. To start rapid growth by multiplication, we must encourage our own local church (be we pastor, layman, or missionary) to reproduce itself in another part of the city or in a neighboring town or village.⁴

Engel and Norton believe that one believer winning another is not enough. They state that "it is a demonstrated principle of church growth that Christianity gains in a society only to the extent that the number of existing churches is multiplied. Multiplication of new congregations of believers, then, is the normal and expected output of a healthy body."⁵

Dr. Charles L. Chaney, a Southern Baptist, wrestles with the arguments against starting new churches and identifies the movement as "the new Anti-Missionism." He maintains that the anti-mission spirit takes one of three forms. (1) The Common Sense Syndrome--which is the argument that there are already too many small struggling churches. (2) Jackhylitus---which is not meant to disparage the great job Jack Hyles is doing but describes the feeling among some that small churches are inferior and cannot compare in many areas to the large growing churches. (3) <u>The One-for-One Strategy</u>--which can be summarized in the goal of having one large strong church in each city and that is sufficient."[6]

Concerning the problem of the large church versus the small church (an issue of concern today), Dr. Chaney states:

> Let me remind you that big churches come from little churches--nowhere else. That is true in two ways. All big churches were at one time small. But, every large church is composed of hundreds of Christians that were won to Christ in small churches. Every church in the SBC with more than 3,000 members is surrounded by hundreds of smaller churches that share Christ in every socio-economic stratum of the society. Hundreds of little Baptist churches preaching the Gospel to all different people that make up our society make large churches more likely to occur.[7]

Dr. Chaney concludes his inspiring challenge by encouraging each church to plan to begin another church or chapel by the end of 1978.[8] The history of missions indicates that specific planning and goal-setting for the multiplication of new churches has not been the norm, at least since the days of Paul. But rather it has been common to assume that church growth will automatically happen without planning for it. Therefore, somewhat like spontaneous combustion, churches will be planted and grow according to God's timetable. As long as the church carries on the whole program of God in the world, church growth really doesn't matter.[9] McGavran challenges this as a common assumption that is a serious mistake, and adds that "church growth seldom comes without bold plans for it."[10]

> If we believe that expansion is the principal mission of the Church and that all secondary activities should contribute toward this goal, we must make definite plans to reach the desired objectives and measure our progress toward them. Without plans it is possible to float aimlessly, swept along by the currents of popular ideas or by many other pressures or influences.[11]

McGavran adds, "Only those who disregard the evidence can believe that church growth is a by-product of multi-faceted mission. The assumption is contrary to the New Testament practice."[12] Several authors, including Weld,

Notes

McGavran, Michael Green, Roland Allen and others, refer to the strategy that the apostle Paul used in his church planting endeavors. The apostle Paul concentrated his efforts on cities, which were centers of communication, transportation, and commerce. Paul planned to begin churches. He would often go to the synagogue seeking to win his Jewish countrymen first (Acts 13:5-Salamis; Acts 13:14-Pisidian Antioch; Acts 14:1-Iconium; Acts 17:1,2-Thessalonica; Acts 18:4-Corinth). Paul gained a hearing with the Jews who attended the synagogues and later continued with the Gentiles (God-fearers) who also had heard of him and his message. As the Scripture indicates, before Paul reached Thessalonica he had been practicing his plan for starting churches, to the point where Acts 17:2 records, "And according to Paul's <u>custom</u>, he went to them, and for three Sabbaths reasoned with them from the Scriptures" (NASB, underline added).

Referring to the rapid and wide expansion of the early church, Roland Allen emphasizes, "spontaneous expansion," although he does explain the issue of organization as well.

> The Church expanded simply by organizing these little groups early disciples as they were converted, handing on to them the organization which she had received from her first founders. It was itself a unity composed for a multitude of little churches, any one of which could propagate itself, and consequently the reception of any new group of Christians was a simple matter. By a simple act the new group was brought into the unity of the Church, and equipped, as its predecessors had been equipped, not only with all the spiritual power and authority necessary for its own life as an organized unity, but also with all the authority needed to repeat the same process whenever one of its members might convert men in any new village or town.[13]

The Bible churches are having a negative influence on independent fundamental churches today. Most of them maintain that edification is the primary aim or controlling purpose of the church. They deny that soul-winning or evangelism is its over-riding aim.

McGavran, whose concern and interest is clearly the multiplication of new churches, believes the sequence of the Great Commission to "make disciples of all nations" precedes "training them to observe all," he argues:

> Only churches which exist can be perfected.

Only babies who have been born can be educated. Only where practicing Christians form sizable minorities of their societies can they expect their presence seriously to influence the social, economic, and political structures. The Church must, indeed, "teach them all things," but first she must have at least some Christians and some congregations.[14]

CONCLUSION

Therefore, since the purpose of the Great Commission is finalized in the planting of a New Testament church, those church planters who establish a church are not doing something that is spectacular or overwhelmingly unique. They are simply carrying out the command of Jesus Christ that is given to all.

Also, church planters should not be thought of as devisive (sapping strength from existing churches) nor selfish (wanting to control a church so they plant their own) nor too independent (unwilling to take an existing pulpit). They should be thought of as those who are employing the most biblical methods to reach the sprawling metropolitan areas of the United States. Since we want to effectively reach the United States, we should use the most effective evangelistic tool we can find. All forms of evangelism have their place, but the most effective method is to plant a New Testament church in every section of every city of the United States.

FOOTNOTES

1. Virgil Gerber, <u>God's Way to Keep a Church Going and Growing</u> (Glendale, CA: Regal Books, 1973), p. 18.

2. <u>Ibid</u>., p. 17.

3. Orlando E. Costas, <u>The Church and Its Mission: A Shattering Critique from the Third World</u> (Wheaton, Illinois: Tyndale House, 1974), p. 120.

4. Paul Davis, "Church Multiplication," <u>Church Growth Bulletin</u>, vol. 2, no. 1 (September 1965), p. 92.

5. James F. Engel and H. Wilbert Norton, <u>What's Gone Wrong With the Harvest? A Communication Strategy for the Church and World Evangelism</u> (Grand Rapids: Zondervan, 1975), pp. 143, 144.

6. Charles L. Chaney, "A New Day for New Churches," <u>Church Growth Bulletin</u>, vol. 2, no. 1 (September 1965), pp. 512-516.

7. <u>Ibid.</u>, p. 515.

8. <u>Ibid.</u>, p. 516.

9. Donald A. McGavran, <u>Understanding Church Growth</u> (Grand Rapids: William B. Eerdmans, 1970), p. 354.

10. <u>Ibid.</u>

11. Wayne Weld and Donald McGavran, <u>Principles of Church Growth</u> (South Pasadena, California: William Carey Library, 1974), pp. 15-20.

12. McGavran, <u>Understanding</u>, p. 356.

13. Roland Allen, <u>The Spontaneous Expansion of the Church</u> (Grand Rapids: William B. Eerdmans, 1962), p. 143.

14. McGavran, <u>Understanding</u>, p. 359.

Questions For Review

1. The first aspect of the Great Commission is planting churches.   True   False

2. God's primary method of evangelism in this age is church planting.   True   False

3. The Great Commission as it appears in John gives us our strategy for church planting.   True   False

4. The goal of New Testament evangelism is to produce responsible and reproducing Christians and churches.   True   False

5. Church planting is a comparatively recent phenomeon.   True   False

6. The three-fold command of the Great Commission is fulfilled by the New Testament church.   True   False

7. It took only four generations to start churches in every known pagan center after the dispersion of Acts 8.   True   False

8. The best way for a church to grow is to be active in reproducing itself.   True   False

9. The principle of multiplication which produces the fastest growth of Christianity is one believer reaching another and beginning the chain of multiplication.   True   False

10. Jackhylitus has started more churches in southeast Asia during the past decade than the entire Methodist missionary force in that area using the principle of indigenous evangelism.   True   False

11. The One-for-One Strategy can be summarized in the goal of one super church per city.   True   False

12. Church growth will automatically happen without planning for it.   True   False

13. In today's world, Bible churches are positively influencing fundamentalist churches to evangelism.   True   False

14. Church planters by nature tend to be divisive, selfish and too independent.   True   False

15. Evangelism is the overriding aim of the church.   True   False

CHAPTER 3

CHURCH PLANTING AND THE NATURE OF A CHURCH

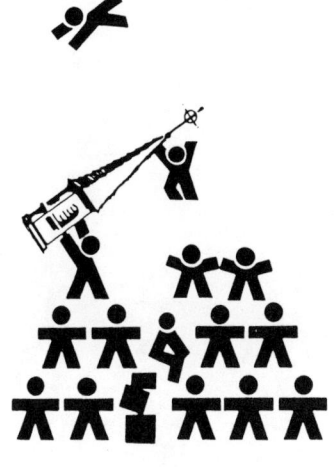

When a church planter begins a local church, he should realize that only Jesus Christ can establish a New Testament church. Many men have attempted to plant a church but failed because there was never the life of God in the organization. It was as if the body had been stillborn. Some new churches have had elections for its officers or there was a nucleus of believers, but the organization was not a New Testament church. The church planter should know what makes up a New Testament church so that it may thrive, and if it dies; at least the church planter knew what was wrong. This chapter discusses the composition and nature of a local church so that the church planter will have guidance in planning its birth and growth.

But there is a second reason for the church planter to know his ecclesiology. The end product (church) is a result of his doctrine. So if his theology of the church is right, then he will properly plant and develop it to maturity.

Those who feel the Bible church is biblical, claim the aim of the church is first biblical education (Eph. 4: 11,12), so the people who are grounded in the Bible will win souls, which is the second priority of the church. If this were true, a church would be planted through Bible study groups with an emphasis on getting people into the Word of God. There is nothing wrong with getting lost people into the Word and founding a church on Bible study groups, but there is a better way which is to reverse the order (Matt. 28:19,20).

Those who feel the church is expressed in Body Life fellowship (kononia) will attempt to build up people and bring in others that they may experience group fellowship and come to know Christ. Once again fellowship is a good aim because it builds up Christians and provides a place to produce New Testament maturity, but the church planter has evangelistic priorities that are greater.

Of course a church is not the building nor is any gathering of Christians a church, just because they call themselves by that title. The word _ecclesia_ in the New Testament meant "assembly" and any church must be a gathering of those who are Christians. The term _ecclesia_, mentioned 114 times in the New Testament, could have been better translated in our Bible as "assembly." Whenever we think of the term <u>church</u>, let us always primarily concern ourselves with the people who are assembled in the name of the Lord.

> A church is an assembly of baptized believers, in whom Christ dwells, under the discipline of the Word of God, organized for evangelism, education, fellowship and worship; administering the ordinances and reflecting the spiritual gifts.

The church planter is performing the highest spiritual function given a pastor, he is bringing together a group of people that will be recognized as the body of the Lord Jesus Christ on earth. The Holy Spirit will dwell there (1 Cor. 3:16) and it will be called a candlestick (Rev. 1:20, 2:1) it will have the presence of Christ (Rev. 2:5) and will be a mystery (Eph. 3:1-10).

1. <u>A church is an assembly of baptized believers</u>. The first criterion for a New Testament church is an assembly of those who have been scripturally baptized according to the purpose and plan of the New Testament. On the day of Pentecost, those who were saved were immediately baptized and they were added to the church. "Then they that gladly received his word were baptized: and the same day there were added unto them about three thousand souls" (Acts 2:41). Baptism became more than an initiatory rite into a local church; it is a symbol portraying the ultimate meaning of the Lord's death. The church is the body of Christ (Eph. 1:22,23). When He hung on Calvary, sinners were placed into the body of Christ, and when Christ suffered vicariously, the penalty of their sins was propitiated because they were in Jesus Christ. Individuals were identified with Christ in His death, burial and resurrection (Rom. 6:4-6). And, as a result, when Christ died, we died with Him: "I am crucified with Christ: nevertheless I live; yet not I, but Christ liveth in me" (Gal. 2:20). Since we were identified with Christ's body at salvation, the symbolism should be carried out when one enters the church, the body of Christ. He is placed into a pool of water as a symbol of being placed in the grave, identified with Christ in His death, burial and resurrection. All people in a New Testament church should profess to be Christians and have been identified with Christ in His work on Calvary.

There will be some in the church who are not saved, as was the case in New Testament times (Acts 8:13-23). However, all should be accepted into the church upon their profession of faith. The church is an assembly of <u>believers</u>,

Notes

and when the church is made up of unbelievers it is no longer a New Testament church.

When is a new church ready to baptize members? Not until it is recognized as a church by Jesus Christ. Obviously, men do not know the exact time when God recognizes as a church a group of people who call themselves a church. Therefore, a chartering or organizing service is held so men can recognize what God has recognized. After men recognize that God has called a group of people together to be a church, then that church can properly baptize candidates.

Actually, the author recommends that an old church document be used in chartering a church that begins, "We the undersigned." This document recognizes congregational authority, for it is the assembled people who give credibility to the new church. A visiting minister leads the new church congregation to recognize that they meet the New Testament marks of a church and he leads them in organizing themselves into a church.

What keeps a group of people from becoming a New Testament church?

1. Wrong doctrine.
2. Unbiblical leadership.
3. Unsaved members.
4. Organized for the wrong purpose.
5. Incorporation of obvious sin/sinners into the new church.

---

2. <u>The unique presence of Jesus Christ dwells in a church</u>. The church is more than an organization; it is an organism and its life is Jesus Christ. He dwells in the midst of His people. "For where two or three are gathered together in my name, there am I in the midst of them" (Matt. 18:20). Christ walked through the seven churches in the book of Revelation and commended them for their good works (Rev. 2:3) and rebuked them for their sin and false doctrine (Rev. 2:1). When Christ rebuked the churches in the book of Revelation He threatened to take away their candlestick (Rev. 2:5), which would have been removing the presence of Jesus Christ from the people. When Christ is present in a New Testament church, it is similar to the shekinah glory cloud coming upon the Old Testament Temple. If a group of people have Jesus Christ dwelling in their midst, they are a New Testament church.

Notes

> **Evidence that a church is indwelt by Jesus Christ.**
>
> 1. Souls are being saved.
> 2. Word of God is preached with power.
> 3. Spirit of love.
> 4. Fellowship that builds up Christians.
> 5. The mature preacher can sense the presence of God in the church.

3. <u>A church must be under the ministry of the Word of God.</u> One of the first religious exercises of the New Testament church after the day of Pentecost was "And they continued steadfastly in the apostles' doctrine" (Acts 2:42). Doctrinal purity is essential for a New Testament church.

When an organizational problem came up in the early church, the apostles realized that they could not waste time waiting on tables when they should be giving themselves to the Word of God (Acts 6:4). A local church must place itself under the authority of God by placing itself under the discipline of the Word of God.

When the minister gives a positive proclamation of the Word of God, this is <u>positive discipline</u>, leading to correct life and belief. When the minister rebukes a congregation for their sin, this is <u>negative discipline</u>, just as a parent rebukes a child for going too near the fire. Sometimes a parent rebukes by the rod. The purpose of discipline is the positive growth and negative correction of the child. The purpose of discipline by the Word of God is the positive growth and negative correction of the New Testament church.

Martin Luther said that one of the characteristics of a church was the correct preaching and teaching of the Word of God. Obviously, a church cannot come into existence without the Bible, for it must be the basis of belief by each member in the new church and corporately they must pledge their allegiance to it.

Actually there is a close identity among the following three; the Bible, the church and the Living Christ. When a person is correct on these three doctines, he is probably correct on all the others. The Bible is the most important aspect of Christianity for it is the objective expression of Jesus Christ, yet the Bible is just a history book without its primary character, Jesus Christ the Son of God. The church is the assembly of Christians, but it is more than a gathering, the vitality of a church is Jesus

Christ who dwells in the church because it is called His body. Therefore, the distinguishing mark of a New Testament church is its allegiance to the Bible.

The church planter must be concerned that the group he is organizing becomes a New Testament church. Therefore, he has four priorities. First, he must be concerned about doctrinal purity of the church's doctrinal statement. (see appendix). But many groups have started with a correct doctrinal statement but did not become "life infilled" because they never became a church. Second, the church planter must see that he preaches and teaches the whole Word of God to the church as a whole and to each individual as a member. Here the church planter must remember the awesome responsibility of a pastor, i.e. that his people's spiritual life is dependent upon his ministry. But here the church planter must realize the actual spiritual existence of the new church depends upon his spiritual ministry. The third aspect involves the corporate application of the Word of God to the church. Therefore, the church planter will spend more time teaching biblical church polity to a new church than will the average pastor. The fourth priority involves applying the Bible to the individual lives of the church members. Everyone should be concerned that his part in establishing the new church is "Spirit-led" and "Bible-based."

What will keep a group of people from becoming a New Testament church?

1. Ignorance of biblical church polity.
2. Wrong doctrinal statement.
3. Unbiblical ministry by church planter.
4. Lack of obedience by Christians to the Word.

---

4. <u>A church must be organized to carry out the Great Commission.</u> The purpose of a church is more than a "back-slapping fellowship" of mutual friends. In the early church they "ceased not to teach and preach Jesus Christ" (Acts 5:42). Since the church believed that everyone was lost, it also believed that everyone must receive an honest hearing of the gospel. The church in Jerusalem carried the gospel to every home so that its persecutors could say, "Ye have filled Jerusalem with your doctrine" (Acts 5:28). The early disciples were carrying out the Great Commission. The first obligation upon a church is evangelism. The second requirement was education; it had

Notes

to indoctrinate the new Christian into the faith. The last part of the Great Commission reinforced this belief: "Teaching them to observe all things whatsoever I have commanded you" (Matt. 28:20).

The church planter must examine his motives for establishing a church. If he wants to evangelize an area and win souls to Christ, God will bless his endeavors. If all other things are equal, then the organization of people will become a church.

The techniques in starting the church are not as important as the compelling desire by the church planter to win souls. Some new works begin off a church split and never become a New Testament church because their main purpose might be to retaliate against the other group or just to be doctrinally pure (the desire to be doctrinally correct is not a sufficient basis to become a New Testament church). Some new works begin as a Bible study group and eventually fail. Their purpose was not to win people to Christ. Yet, many new churches are successfully begun by Bible study groups because their desire is to win souls to Christ.

When the author conducts a chartering/organizing service, he always asks, "How many have been saved since this new church has been meeting together?" If the answer is none, then he has right to doubt if the new group has the annointing of God and is a New Testament church. He has organized over 30 new churches and on three specific occasions no one had been saved in the church when it was organized. Today, all three churches are out of existence, perhaps giving evidence that they were not a church in the first place and the author should not have organized them.

5. <u>A church exercises the ordinances</u>. Two ordinances are given to the church, baptism and the Lord's Table. These are to be celebrated by the church when it assembles together. Even though the ordinances are given for personal edification and testimony, an individual does not partake of these apart from the church.

The church planter does not serve the Lord's Table nor baptize until his new church is chartered as a New Testament church. Since they are ordinances, he cannot exercise them until his new organization is a church.

However, there are some exceptions. If he is sponsored by a mother church and the new group is considered an extension of the sponsoring church, then he can administer the ordinances under their authority. Also, if the church planter is in a foreign culture and realizes there will be a long period of time before he can plant a church, he can baptize new converts under the authority of the sponsoring church that sent him to the field.

The church planter should not be to lose in applying this exception to all situations. Baptism is a testimony of a new converts' conversion, but is is also a symbol of his identification with the local body of the church. If he treats baptism with the respect that God has for its symbolic representation, his people will also treat it and the new church with reverence.

6. <u>A church reflects the spiritual gifts</u>. Not every group of Christians is destined to grow into a church. A group of people must be properly baptized, under the Word of God and organized for God's priorities. God then raises up leadership to bring the church into existence. These leaders must have the "spiritual gifts" (1 Cor. 12; Rom. 12; Eph. 4). God gives gifted men to a church, and when the leaders appear, it is an indication God wants the people to organize into a New Testament church. "God hath set some in the church, first apostles, secondarily prophets, thirdly teachers" (1 Cor. 12:28). "And he gave some apostles, and some prophets, and some evangelists, and some pastors and teachers" (Eph. 4:11).

A church must recognize its' spiritual gifts by recognizing its men to fill the spiritual office of pastor and deacons. When a new congregation will not follow biblical leadership, it will not become a New Testament church. It cannot abuse its leaders by ignoring them or rejecting them. A congregation ignores its leaders by not helping with soul-winning visitation, not praying, etc. It rejects its leaders by voting against them or the programs they suggest.

CONCLUSION

The church planter must know his ecclesiology if he would plant a New Testament church. Jeff Winstead testified that he was not prepared to plant a church when he finished an interdenominational Bible School. However, after graduating from Liberty Baptist Seminary he felt prepared to start a church because he knew the nature of the church he would start, how he would baptize, how he would run its business; but most important, he understood the priority of soul-winning evangelism. Jeff Winstead planted Harvest Baptist Church, Hagerstown, Maryland, in the summer of 1981 and averaged over 200 in attendance by November with an average offering of over $2,000 a week income.

Questions for Review

1. The church you establish will determine your ecclesiology. — True False

2. A Bible church is any church committed to the inerrancy and inspiration of the Scriptures. — True False

3. Members of a body life church emphasis group fellowship. — True False

4. The highest spiritual function given a pastor is to plant a new church. — True False

5. Acts 8:13-23 teaches that it is permittable to allow unsaved people to join a church. — True False

6. Church members should be encouraged to follow the Lord in baptism because of its symbolic meaning. — True False

7. The church is an organization and an organism. — True False

8. A church should begin baptizing its converts the first Sunday it meets. — True False

9. The church symbolically began when the shekinah glory entered Solomon's Temple. — True False

10. The pastor of a new church must preach both the positive and negative discipline of the Word of God. — True False

11. If a pastor is correct on bibliogy, ecclesiology and Christology he will be correct on most other doctrines. — True False

12. The verses which explain the purpose and strategy of the church is Eph. 4:11,12. — True False

13. The church planter should examine his motives in starting a church because some men plant good churches with the wrong motives. — True False

14. The church has only three ordinances, baptism, church chartering and the Lord's Supper. — True False

15. Baptism is not that important in the light of evangelism and church planting. — True False

16. If a group is a New Testament church, God will raise up gifted leaders. — True False

CHAPTER 4

THE ROLE OF THE CHURCH PLANTER

In the past ten years the author has witnessed a great deal of church planting. Many people say one of the renewed reasons for church planting by many fundamental/conservative groups is the national attention given church growth through media exposure to the large church movement and the rapid growth of such groups as the Baptist Bible Fellowship (BBF). The BBF has been more effective in church planting than most other groups.

As a result, many men have tried to plant a church only to fail. The reasons for failure are as diverse as the personality of those who have attempted to plant a church. Some of the reasons are as follows.

1. Lack of financing
2. Lack of biblical training
3. Lack of character in church planter
4. Lack of strategy in church planting
5. Lack of purity in church planter
6. Lack of spiritual maturity in church planter
7. Lack of understanding ecclesiology

All these reasons have crippled some new churches but the author feels that the two major reasons for failure are lack of spiritual maturity and lack of ecclesiology. When the church planter does not know the role that a new pastor should assume, nor the biblical role of a church planter, it is a lack of ecclesiology that will harm his church. Perhaps his lack of maturing is one reason why he is trying to plant a church without proper tools. Hence, the main problem in planting a new church is not what the leader does not do, or does not know, but what he has not become.

This chapter deals with the role of the church planter, what he must become. The full blessing of God depends on how the church planter fills these rolls.

1. His gift	At salvation
2. His calling	Perhaps after conversion
3. His office	Voted by congregation

The church planter was given his spiritual gifts embyronically at conversion, even though they may not come to light until a later time. His call to the ministry probably come at a point after his conversion.

Notes

The <u>office</u> of minister is given to him by vote of the congregation. These three aspects of ministry will be dealt with in this chapter.

I.   THE GIFT OF CHURCH PLANTING

Is there a spiritual gift to plant churches? If there is, then church planting is raised to one of the highest ministries in Christianity. If it is not a spiritual gift, then the church planter must use all the spiritual resources available to him, and apply every spiritual gift to his endeavor of planting a church.

The spiritual gift that comes closest to planting a church is the evangelist, referred to more as the gifted man (Eph. 4:11), rather than just listed among the spirtual gifts of the New Testament. This gift is usually applied to the city-wide, or local church evangelist who holds evangelistic crusades. Whereas the person who holds evangelistic crusades may have this gift, that is not its best expression. The foreign or home missionary who preaches the gospel in unevangelized areas with a view of establishing churches last fulfills the gift of an evangelist. When applied in this manner, the church planter must have the gift of evangelism.

The term evangelist is only mentioned three times in the New Testament. The first is in Acts 21:8 where Philip, chosen in Acts 6 to be a deacon, is named an evangelist. Philip was called an evangelist because he was carrying out the Great Commission in a unique way. The other references are 2 Tim. 4:5, where Timothy is told to do the work of an evangelist, and Eph. 4:11, where the gift of an evangelist is listed. Since very little is known about the evagelist, we should not read into Scripture the modern-day practices of city-wide evangelists.

The root meaning of the term evangelist is to bring good tidings, or to gospelize. The evangelist brings the gospel message. He usually goes to areas that have never been evangelized and preaches the gospel. Philip did this in both Samaria and with the Ethiopian eunuch in the desert.

In listing the offices (gifts) in the church, the evangelist stands between the apostle and the pastor (Eph. 4:11). This implies that the evangelist is sent forth by the first group and prepares the way for the second group. He is sent by the apostles and prophets (those who established the church by writing revelation) and he prepares the way for the pastor who shepherds the flock. Therefore, it appears the evangelist uses his gifts to plant churches.

Philip is the classic example of the evangelist. He

was a pioneer who went to unevangelized areas. He preached the gospel in Samaria (Acts 8:5), Gaza (Acts 8:27), and in his new home (Acts 8:40). His ministry was an itinerant one--he went from place to place, even into the desert to talk with one man, the Ethiopian eunuch. He baptized his converts, therefore, he might be compared to a modern-day foreign missionary or church planter.

An evangelist may or may not be an office, no one knows for sure. But we know the evangelist is a gift which implies a function. Therefore, the person with the gift of evangelism can have a special ability to win people to Christ, more so than the average Christian. This is also reenforced by the fact that spiritual gifts are both qualitative and quantitative. Some are given more spiritual gifts than others and some are given a greater measure of certain gifts than others. Therefore, the church planter should not only be a multi-gifted individual but he should certainly evidence the gift of evangelism.

Remember, a gift can grow in its function and influence (1 Cor. 12:31). That means the person with the gift of evangelism for church planting can increase his total gift and also increase his productivity to win souls as he faithfully applies the talents he has. The church planter does not have to be a great soul winner when he begins planting the church, but the ability should be embyronic and if it is evident, can be developed.

The gift of evangelism would include a great spiritual burden for lost people, the ability to get them saved (by personal evangelism or pulpit evangelism), and the desire to disciple them into maturity. Therefore, if a man has not been fruitful in winning people to Christ, it is questionable if he has the gift to plant a church. This does not mean a man should stop giving consideration to church planting, but it does mean the potential church planter should immediately give himself to soul winning and demonstrate fruit before he attempts to plant a church. A new church is not organized into existence like beginning a new book store, a new church is born through soul winning.

Besides the gift of evangelism, the church planter should be a multi-gifted individual. Since a person's faithfulness will help him discover new gifts as well as develop his present gifts, the church planter is exhorted to follow God's leading in this matter. He will need the following gifts to plant a church.

Notes

Notes

```
            THE GIFTS OF THE HOLY SPIRIT

     Title                      Function

Pastor-Eph. 4:11           lead the people
Teacher-Eph. 4:11          teach the people
Evangelist (Church
   Planter)-Eph. 4:11      win the lost
Helps-1 Cor. 12:28         servant to the flock
Ministry-Rom. 12:7         meet peoples needs
Administration (Busi-
   ness) 1 Cor. 12:18      administer the church
Ruling (Church leader-
   ship)-Rom. 12:8         leadership
Wisdom-1Cor. 12:8          to make decisions
Knowledge-1 Cor. 12:8      knowledgeable
Faith-1 Cor. 12:9          trust God for results
Prophecy-Rom. 12:6         preach the Word
Giving-Rom. 12:8           money
Exhortation-Rom. 12:8      encourage people
Showing mercy-Rom. 12:8    counsel & understand
Love-Rom. 12:9               others
```

II. THE CALL TO CHURCH PLANTING

The church planter must have a dual calling. First, he must be called into full time Christian work. This is the traditional explanation given to a young man who is separated by God for the ministry. But in a second sense, he must be called to go out and start a church. Since not every minister can start a church, the church planter needs to understand the distinction between the two.

The predominate theological use of the idea of "call" in Scripture is the person who is called into full time service (Acts 13:2,3). However, the Bible also speaks of a call to sanctification (1 Cor. 1:9) and a call to salvation (2 Thess. 1:11, Rom. 1:6, 8:28).

Barnabas and Paul were called of God to full-time Christian service. Remember, even at Paul's conversion it was indicated that he would be a unique servant and messenger to the Gentiles (Acts 9:15-16). However, after 14 years of learning and apprenticeship, by serving Jesus Christ in the church at Damascus, Tarsus and Antioch, Paul was ready to be separated into full-time Christian service. We read the account, "As they ministered to the Lord, and fasted, the Holy Ghost said, Separate me Barnabas and Saul for the work whereunto I have called them" (Acts 13:2). Note that these two men who were called into full-time Christian service were actively involved in serving Jesus Christ. The call did not come to two unconcerned high school boys who were sitting on the last pew in the church. These were active church leaders who were called into full-time Christian service. A second part of the call is that they were to be separated, indicating they were no longer considered laymen. A third part of the call to full-time service was accompanied with self-examination and searching the mind of the Lord. Barnabas and Saul were fasting and praying to the Lord when they were called. Notice the verse begins, "as." They were in the process of serving the Lord when they were called. A last part of the call is that it came from the Holy Spirit. No man can issue the call to himself. He can desire the office of a bishop (I Tim. 3:7), but the call of God comes from the Holy Spirit.

When Paul wrote to the Romans he identified himself as "Paul, a servant of Jesus Christ, called to be an apostle" (Rom. 1:1). In the same manner, every minister of Jesus Christ can identify himself as one who is called to serve Jesus Christ.

When the author attends an ordination service he always asks the candidate the following question, "What is the call of God and how do you know that you have it?" If a candidate cannot identify the call of God and convince the council that he has been called to full-time Christian service, then we should not ordain him no matter how much theological knowledge he has. Ordination is a serious matter and no one should have "hands laid on him" if there is not absolute assurance that he has been called into full-time Christian service.

Once a young man answered the question by indicating the command in Scripture was the call of God. He noted since Jesus had commanded to go and preach the gospel to everyone, he should do so. This answer was not enough. Surely the call of God is based on the command of Scripture. But, the command of God is given to everyone. Every Christian should preach the gospel to all people. That is the basis for the call. But the call to full-time

Notes

Christian service is more than the command of Scripture, it is a unique experience that only those who have been set aside by Jesus Christ have received. The command of Scripture is to everyone, the call of God is more particular, it is only to the recipients.

Then the candidate gave a second basis for the call of God. He said the call of God was the need of people to hear the gospel. He went on to indicate that there were thousands of needy people in the city who needed to get saved. Once again the candidate had to be corrected. The need is an obligation upon every Christian, but the need alone is not the call. Every Christian meets needy people every day of his life, but this does not constitute a call to full-time Christian service. The call is based upon the need of people to hear the gospel, but the call of God to full-time Christian service is a unique experience that goes beyond the obligation of every Christian.

Therefore the call to full-time Christian service can be described in three ways: first desire, second burden, and third by fruit.

1. <u>The call of God begins with a burden.</u> Several of the Old Testament prophets indicated that their message was the burden of the Lord (Mal. 1:1; Hab. 1:1). A burden is an obligation or a compulsion. A young man who is called into full-time Christian service has a burden or a compulsion to serve Jesus Christ. The need of lost people adds to the burden he gets from Scripture, but the burden is a unique and inner assurance that he must serve Jesus Christ with all of his life.

The call to full-time Christian service has no alternative God does not say to a young person I will call you to serve me full-time if you cannot get a better job. The call to full-time Christian service carries the weight of "ought" or "must." When a young person is called into full-time Christian service, he must obey, there is no alternative.

2. <u>The call to full-time Christian service involves desire.</u> A man knows he is called of God when his greatest desire is to serve Jesus Christ with every part of his life. This involves his will, it is surrendered and he wants to spend all of his time serving Jesus Christ. Usually the call to full-time Christian service comes to those who are actively involved in the bus ministry, teaching Sunday School, or perhaps being a deacon in a local church. They have enjoyed their experience so much that they want to serve God with all of their heart and all of their time.

Jeremiah experienced the burning desire to preach the Word of God. Someone told him he could not preach. He responded, "But His word was in mine heart as a burning fire shut up in my bones, and I was weary with forebearing, and I could not stay (keep quiet)" (Jer. 20:9).

For many years the author has dealt with young men who are studying for full-time Christian service. The ones that delight him the most are those young men who just have to preach when they enter their freshman year. They are willing to preach in children's church, in the rescue mission, or in the nursing homes. When a man has the fire burning in his heart he will sometimes go out into the woods and preach to an empty hillside. This is more than practice, it is preparation for a lifetime of delivering the Word of God.

3. <u>The call of God is evidenced by fruit</u>. When God has put his hand upon a young man and separated him to full-time Christian service, there will be corresponding fruit. Therefore, before a council ordains a young man into the full-time ministry, there should be some evidence that God has used his preaching and teaching of the Word of God. Jesus noted, "Ye have not chosen me, but I have chosen you and ordained you that ye should go and bring forth fruit, and that your fruit should remain" (John 15:16). The word *ordain* means to lay hands upon, and Jesus was indicating that He had chosen people and put His hands upon them to bring forth fruit.

The symbolic laying on of hands at an ordination service indicates that God has put His spirit and influence on the ministry of a young man. When he has preached, people have gotten saved. When he has taught the Word of God, people have been followers of Jesus Christ.

Some people are called immediately when they are converted. They know when they pray for conversion, God also wants them to be a minister of the Gospel. Recently in two ministerial classes at Liberty Baptist Schools, I asked for a show of hands on this subject. In both of the classes, only about 10 percent of the students lifted a hand to indicate that they were called into full-time Christian service at the same time they were saved. That meant that most of the young people were called into full-time Christian service at some later time in their Christian life.

Some people receive a sudden and clear call to the ministry. They have been serving Jesus Christ, but by one experience or in one sermon, God impressed upon them to be a full-time Christian servant. Their call to full-time

Notes

Christian service became one event that was life changing. They surrendered for full-time Christian service and from that moment on, they were no longer the same. This is usually evidenced by going forward in a service. On the other hand, the call of God has come gradually to many other servants. They begin to feel a burden for the ministry as they serve the Lord. Each time they preached or taught, their desire grew to teach or preach again. Their call to full-time Christian ministry was a gradual call. The same classes were asked, "Did your call to full-time ministry come suddenly or gradually over a long period of time?" Again about 10 percent were called suddenly, the other 90 percent received the call to full-time service gradually.

1. A strong and abiding desire for the work, springing from a supreme love of Christ. 1 Tim. 3:1 (eagerness and fixedness of mind and the work belonging to it).
2. A deep and abiding sense of personal weakness and unworthiness. Paul said, "I am the least of the apostles, that am not worthy to be called an apostle."
3. A comfortable hope for needed grace and strength. 2 Cor. 3:4-6 "And such have we through Christ to Godward; not that we are sufficient as of ourselves, but our sufficiency is of God who also hath made us able ministers of the New Testament."
4. High estimate of the office: "a good work."
5. Possession of the necessary learning and power of explaining and enforcing truth, or the means and desire of acquiring them. Is. 11:2,3; Matt. 4:18-20 "Follow me and I will make you fishers of men."
6. The consent and approval of God's people. Acts 6:1-6.
7. God's direct leadership in Scripture revealing His will.
8. A conviction of duty. "Immediately I conferred not with flesh and blood." "Necessity is laid upon me, yea, woe is unto me, if I preach not the gospel." Gal. 1:16; Acts 26:19; 1 Cor. 9:16.

If a "call" is real it will gain strength by time and test.*

*Plumer, William S., <u>Pastoral Theology</u>, Harper & Brothers: New York, N.Y., 1874, pp. 24-35.

III. THE OFFICE OF PASTOR

The church planter must be sure of the role of a pastor before he begins the church. If the wrong authority is given to the deacons or to the congregation, the new church may come into existence, but it will be crippled for life. Therefore, the church planter must understand his role and assume it with biblical authority.

Every church is led by Christ if it is a New Testament church. "He is the head of the body, the church;

who is the beginning, the first-born from the dead, that in all things he might have the pre-eminence" (Col. 1:18). When the presence of Christ leaves a church and He is no longer the ruler, we may call the organization a church but it is not an organic church according to the biblical use of the term.

The final seat of authority in church government rests in the congregation as the people are led by the Spirit of Christ. The apostle Paul encouraged the Philippian believers to continue in and strengthen their unity as a church (Phil. 2:1-2) and pleaded with the Corinthians that they do everything within their power to correct and prevent divisions that existed in their church (1 Cor. 1:10). Because the Holy Spirit works through believers, He is able to freely lead a church when the members are yielded to His direction.

The pastor is the human individual responsible before God for the spiritual welfare of the church (Acts 20:28). At the return of Christ, He will judge and reward pastors according to their faithfulness in leading the church to accomplish the will of God (1 Pet. 5:4). In one sense, everything a church is and does is an extension of the pastor's personal ministry. So much so, that the prophet identifies the similarity between the leader and his followers, "As with the people, so with the priest" (Is. 24:2).

At least seven different terms are used to identify men that filled the office of pastor in New Testament churches. Each of these words contributes toward a fuller understanding of the nature of the pastor's office.

1. <u>Elder</u>. The first term used especially in the Jerusalem church was <u>elder</u> (Acts 11:30). The term <u>elder</u> appears over twenty additional times in the New Testament. Perhaps it was brought over from the Old Testament synogogue of those who were respected for their maturity and wisdom. The book of Proverbs gives admonition to heed those who can make wise decisions. While chronological age was certainly a consideration in identifying a man as an elder, the real emphasis is on wisdom and spiritual maturity. It is not advisable to place a young convert, even if he is saved late in life, in a position of leadership without his first being given the opportunity to gain the spiritual maturity. In listing the qualifications of a pastor, the apostle Paul warned, "Not a novice, lest being lifted up with pride he fall into the condemnation of the devil" (1 Tim. 3:6). Therefore, the church planter

Notes

who has just graduated from school will have to demonstrate his maturity as he plants a church.

The term elder is often used in the plural (cf. Jas. 5:14; Tit. 1:5; 1 Pet. 5:1; Acts 20:17), supporting the idea of a plurality of elders in a single local church. In our churches we have senior ministers, youth pastors, ministers of music and directors of Christian education, all considered pastors. Even in the New Testament where many elders existed in one church, there seems to be a hierarchy of elders. There were many elders in the church of Jerusalem, but James was recognized above the others as spokesman, he had even more authority than the apostles (Acts 15:2,13,22). There were many elders at the Ephesian church (Acts 20:17) but Jesus addressed His comments to a single leader of that church (Rev. 2:1), presumably this leader was recognized by other pastors as the leader among leaders. The church planter will be the only elder in the new church that he plants. He will make plans to expand his staff with time. Even then he should plan to hire men who are mature and give evidence of gifts where he is weak.

2. Bishop. The term bishop is also used to describe the office of pastor and the man who fills it. The term is translated overseers in Acts 20:28 and is used in four other times as bishop (Phil. 1:1, 1 Tim. 3:2, Tit. 1:7, 1 Pet. 2:25). The emphasis of bishop seems to be "one who takes the oversight of a church," or the office of manager, superintendent or chief executive officer of the church. It is largely an administrative term used to identify the work of this church leader. The pastor is one who is to lead the church (Heb. 13:7,17). This term was used in Greek culture to identify the agent of the central government sent out to inspect the subject states and govern them. As the apostles used this term to identify the pastor, the members of the church would have understood what was implied. Whereas the term elder implied the character of the pastor, the term bishop implies his ability to organize and administer the church.

The church planter will be the leader of the new flock and will make many decisions, about the church long before there is a church congregation. Some may criticize the pastor for taking too much authority, but the office of bishop assumes the church planter will take the oversight of a flock. A bishop implies leadership. The church planter leads in evangelism, finances, decisions and teaching. Perhaps those who criticize pastoral leadership have psychological problems with self-acceptance, meaning they could never lead others so they attack those who do. Others have problems with pastoral leadership because of tradition, "they did it back home." Of course, that is not the biblical standard. Pastoral leadership is one of the biggest problems facing the church planter, not by those he leads to the Lord but by older Christians who come from churches that did not have biblical government. Therefore, he must teach his new flock the biblical value of the bishop/pastor.

    3. _Pastor_. Probably the term _pastor_ is the most common title used today by conservation Christians to identify their church leader. However, the term _pastor_ is rarely used in the New Testament. This does not mean the title pastor is unimportant. In contrast, it is one of the chief words to reflect his ministry. This is the same word that could be translated "shepherd." As the shepherd of the flock is responsible for the care of the sheep, so the pastor is responsible for the care of his flock (Acts 20:29; 1 Pet. 5:3).

    First, the pastor/shepherd is instructed to "take heed, therefore, unto yourselves, and to all the flock" (Acts 20:28). This makes the pastor responsible to watch over others to meet their needs. Sometimes a church member will become discouraged or backslidden. The pastor is the person best able to encourage that person so he remains faithful or comes back into fellowship with the Lord.

    Three times Jesus reminded Peter of his pastoral shepherding responsibility to feed the flock (Jn. 21:15,16,17). This mainly involves the teaching ministry of the pastor. To better accomplish this task, many pastors give leadership to such programs as Sunday School, youth clubs, or Bible study groups. Even when the pastor has delegated his ministry in part to others, he remains responsible before God for the feeding of the flock (Acts 20:28). This is why a pastor should be involved in the selection of the curriculum used in his Sunday School and why teachers should cooperate with him. In a very real sense, the Sunday School teacher is an undershepherd of that part of the flock to which they are assigned.

    Pastors should also protect their flock. The apostle Paul recognized that "grievous wolves" would come from the outside and gain control in the church if the flock was not carefully guarded (Acts 20:29). Sometimes, good men in the church may change and thus become dangerous to the security of the church (Acts 20:30). In both cases, the chief responsibility of protecting the flock falls on the pastor. Many times a pastor may be misunderstood when he insists upon certain spiritual standards or certain emphasis in special music or guest preachers. Actually, he may be attempting to protect those Christians who do not understand the total ministry that may be best for the church.

    Most conservative churches use the term _pastor_ to identify their church leader for cultural reasons. Often, the pastor who is a recent graduate is younger than

Notes

deacons, so the title "elder" seems unappropriate. The term bishop has come to refer to a nonbiblical ecclesiastical hierarchy, thus becoming unsuitable for popular use in a Bible-believing church.

The term elder and bishop are used interchangeable in Titus 1:5-7 and Acts 20:17-28, implying these are two functions of the same office. A person grows into becoming an elder, but learns how to function as a bishop.

```
                    NAMING THE PASTOR
             Acts 20:17-31        1 Pet. 5:1-4
  Elder      20:17                5:1 (called elder)
  Bishop     20:28 (overseers)    5:2 (taking oversight)
  Pastor     20:28 (to feed)      5:2 (feed the flock)
```

4. Preacher. The term preacher implies a public proclamation of the gospel. Noah was the first to preach (1 Pet. 2:5), although Enoch's prophesying may also have involved preaching (Jude 14). Preaching is often defined as "the communication of the Word of God with persuasion through the personality." The pastor is the man God has called to proclaim His message in the church. In preaching, the pastor seeks to accomplish those things. "But he that prophesieth speaketh unto men to edification, and exhortation, and comfort" (1 Cor. 14:3).

The author opened a closed church by a complete reorganization, hence he planted a church but did not have to construct a building (Westminster Presybterian Church, Savannah, GA). The people called him preacher, giving evidence that the new church was built on preaching. The church planter must be known for preaching.

5. Teacher. The teaching ministry is referred to some 97 times in the New Testament. The pastor was given the dual gift of "shepherding/teacher" (Eph. 4:11). There is no Greek word in Ephesians 4:11 for and, implying all pastors also had the gift of teaching. This gift was exercised in the church from its beginning (Acts 2:42). Note, Jesus had left His disciples with a "teaching commission" (Mt. 28:19-20). Their obedient response is seen in the biblical record. "And daily in the temple, and in every house, they ceased not to teach and preach Jesus Christ" (Acts 5:42).

The twofold task faces the church planter. First, he must ground the young Christians in the faith, this involves teaching. Second, he must ground the young congregation in the unique church polity that will make them successful. Again, this involves teaching.

6. **Servant**. The term <u>doulos</u>, usually translated "servant" in our Bibles, might better be translated "slave." Usually the term is used to refer to deacons, but it is also used in connection with pastors (1 Pet. 5:3; 2:16). Pastors are to be servants of the congregation. A pastor must keep sensitive to the poor, downtrodden and underprivileged in the flock if he is to remain effective. As a slave of God he is the servant of the church because the assembly is indwelt by Christ and is His body. Jesus used the slave-master relationship to illustrate our duty to Him. "So ye also, when ye shall have done all these things which are commanded you, say, we are unprofitable servants: we have done that which was our duty to do" (Lk. 17:10).

The church planter must be forceful and authoritative, or else the new church will die in birth pangs. Yet the church planter must be a servant of all in his new congregation. He is a servant to the youngest Christian and the elderly.

7. <u>Steward</u>. A pastor is also to be a steward, who was a slave with the responsibility of overseeing other slaves in the master's house or field. A steward is one who manages what belongs to someone else. The pastor is a steward of the gospel (1 Pet. 4:10) and the church (Tit. 1:7). His chief responsibility was identified by the apostle Paul: "Moreover, it is required in stewards, that a man be found faithful" (1 Cor. 4:2).

The church planter has the difficult task of giving away the organization he has founded. Any businessman who goes out and sacrifices to start a company can run his company as he pleases because it belongs to him. But the church planter is different. He sacrifices to give birth to a church, then realizes the church does not belong to him, it belongs to Jesus Christ. The people he wins to Christ can vote him out. Yet, most church planters invest their lives in the church they plant. There is a growing respect between people and pastor over the years. When both remember the biblical role of the other, then they can have a long and fruitful ministry.

SUMMARY

The church must allow its leaders to lead. The pastorate is a leading office. This does not mean dictatorship, control or even ownership of the property. If the people do not follow, then the failure is with the leader. The deacons/committee must give wisdom and guidance to the pastor and to the congregation. They are a serving office while they work behind the scene, they must work together with pastors and people (1 Cor. 3:9). The congregation has the final seat of authority in the church. They are not leaders, they are sheep which are known for following. Actually, the shepherd of the flock is Jesus Christ who originally gave the church authority for government and today guides the pastor, deacons and congregation in carrying out His will.

THREE KINDS OF CHURCH GOVERNMENT

Kind	Congregational	Representative	Episcopal
Authority	People	Board	Man
Strengths	Church decides together--unity	Stability	Takes fullest advantage of gifted leader
Weaknesses	Lack of direction	Rationalistic	Poor leadership
Philosophy	Democratic	Representative, Republican	Monarchy

THE CHURCH PLANTER

His authority in the church, as God's leader, is a moral and spiritual power, not a legal one. He should exercise leadership. He must refuse to compromise Biblical convictions, even though he should be gracious in attitude, and never be stubborn about personal opinions or desires that do not involve Biblical principles. His authority rests in the power of a godly example, as well as in the fact that he is a Biblical officer (1 Pet. 5:3, Eph. 4:11, 12). However, he is not to be a lord over God's heritage" (1 Pet. 5:1-4). He has no Biblical right to be autocratic, dictatorial or domineering. No man of God, filled with the Spirit, will manifest such an attitude.*

---

*Paul R. Jackson, <u>The Doctrine and Administration of the Church</u>, p. 45.

Questions for Review

1. The Southern Baptist Convention has been the most effective church planting group in the past decade resulting in their large numbers.   True   False

2. Those who start churches usually fail for lack of exxlesiology and personal maturity.   True   False

3. A poor understanding of ecclesiology affects the church planters strategy and organization in the new church.   True   False

4. Some spiritual gifts are given embryonically at conversion, while others spiritual gifts are received later.   True   False

5. The spiritual gift which comes closest to the church planter is the gift of an apostle because he was sent out to start churches.   True   False

6. The New Testament evangelist was one who started churches through city wide crusades.   True   False

7. Philip and Timothy are the only two men identified with the gift of evangelists in the New Testament.   True   False

8. In the list of official gifts in the church, the evangelist stands between the apostle and the pastor.   True   False

9. The church planter must be a successful and proven soul winner before he starts the church.   True   False

10. The church planter does not need to know his gifts before starting a new church.   True   False

11. The call to start a church is distinct from the call to preach.   True   False

12. The need for a church in a town constitutes the call of God to that town.   True   False

13. The call to church planting may begin with a desire to start a church.   True   False

14. The church planter's authority to lead a church is recognized by his church members because he started the church.   True   False

15. Some who criticize pastoral leadership do so because they have a problem with self-acceptance.   True   False

16. One of the most difficult tasks of the church planter is to give away the organization he has founded.   True   False

CHAPTER 5

THE THEOLOGY OF THE CHARTERING SERVICE

The author has been privileged to help organize or charter approximately 30 churches (January 1982). The meeting is usually called an organizational meeting if it is the first meeting of a group of people who organize themselves into a church. Dr. Dallas Billington, pastor, Akron Baptist Temple held tent revival meetings throughout Ohio, and at the end of the week long meeting, he would organize the people into a church. On the other hand, this meeting is called a chartering service when a group of Christians have been in existence and grown large enough so that it can be recognized as a church. Chartering services usually apply to the recognition of a mission Sunday School or recognition of a group of people gathered by the church planter who went to a town with the purpose of starting a church. In the past, chartering had the legal ramifications of state recognition to own property and conduct business.

Today, the church planter should not confuse legal incorporation and the chartering/organizational meeting. The first is a legal step that involves properly filing a state application. The second involves a church service to recognize the spiritual existence of the church.

When a church is incorporated it has the right to own property and other tangible goods, plus operate as a non-profit business. Incorporation is recognition by the state of the legal entity of a group of people and when the church is incorporated; its name is protected so some other group cannot take the identical name.

The chartering/organizational meeting is held to determine if a group of people meet the spiritual criteria of a New Testament church, and if they do, then organize them into the basic aspects of a functioning church.

Can Anyone Begin a Church?

The question is occasionally asked, "What agent/agency does God use to organize a local church?" Some feel that only a New Testament church can constitute another church. They feel this way because of their doctrine of baptism--every person must be baptized by a person who has been properly immersed. This view is called "Landmarkism." Its adherents believe a new group of people cannot begin administering baptism or the Lord's table until they get authority by being organized from a duly constituted New Testament church.

Notes

There are problems with this view. First, the argument becomes continuous in time, and every local church must trace the authority of its baptism back past the mother church to the grandparent church to the great-grandparent church *ad infinitum*. But when a new local congregation meets God's requirement, they become a church. Then they can baptize with the authority of Christ, not the authority of the mother church.

The second argument is the church in Samaria. Philip went to Samaria and preached the gospel, baptizing them (Acts 8:12-17), before the Jerusalem church sent Peter and John down to determine the Samarian church's credibility. Also, the church at Antioch was apparently organized and responsible for a great revival long before the mother church at Jerusalem put its stamp of approval on the new congregation (Acts 11:21-24). So, new churches in the Scriptures began without the vote of approval from another congregation.

Third, Jesus is the agent that founds the church. He called it "my church," meaning a congregation belongs to him. Also, he states, "I will build," indicating that a group of people must be put together by Jesus Christ to qualify for being a local church. The word for church, *Ecclesia*, means "to call out." Jesus calls men to salvation and places them in his body, the church. This is how he builds the church. Christ is the architect, designer, contractor and, finally, he occupies the church. "And hath put all things under His (Christ) feet, and gave Him to be the head over all things to the church, which is the body" (Eph. 1:22-23). Christ also fills the church with his light (John 8:12); hence, it is called a candlestick. Obviously, Christ fills the church with his fulness causing us to say the church is equivalent to Jesus Christ, from beginning to end. Just as the body belongs to the head, Christ is the head of each local body. When Christ does the work, it is his church. Therefore, the organizational meeting is just "recognition day." As the author said at one service, "We're just watching what God is doing. My organizational powers won't make this church any more spiritual...any more powerful...it won't even make this congregation an authentic church. If God has built you, this congregation is now a church."

Landmarkism believes a new local church becomes authentic when it is organized by an existing New Testament church. However, Jesus Christ is the agent who makes a church authentic.

Fourth, many young men have gone out from fundamental colleges and started a successful New Testament church. They just went out to begin a church in obedience to the call of God, relying on the power of God, building on the Word of God.

True, they have been ordained by a New Testament church and sponsored in college by that church. When they went to a new community, their home church considered them "their boy." However, there was no official commissioning service to set them aside for starting the new church. This does not mean the new congregation lacks any spiritual power because there was no official vote by the mother church. Gerald Fleming graduated from Baptist Bible Seminary, Fort Worth and went to Dayton, Ohio, struggling for weeks before a group of people began meeting regularly. Bruce Cummings also graduated from Baptist Bible Seminary, knowing he wanted to start a church somewhere in Ohio or West Virginia. God led him to Massillon, Ohio, and a church of 2,000 evolved; once again, without a sponsoring church.

Other New Testament churches grew out of existing congregations and at a time in their existence, became a church. Curtis Hutson was a part-time postman and pastor in Decatur, Georgia when he read in a discarded issue of The Sword of the Lord that Dr. Jack Hyles baptized over 2,000 converts in one year. Thinking the statistic was a mistake, Hutson went to hear Hyles speak. While listening to Hyles give his famous lecture on soul-winning, Hutson realized two things. First, he determined his was not a church. He determined to go back and preach the Word according to the commandments of Jesus Christ. Second, Hutson determined that he could win souls. The following Saturday, he led three people to Jesus Christ. There has not been a week since that time that Hutson has not led someone to Jesus Christ. The Forest Hills Baptist Church grew and became a true New Testament church without the sponsorship of another congregation.

Fifth, some New Testament churches have started a mission congregation which failed. If there was any magical success to rub off from the mother church, insuring the existence of its children, surely the new church would have had it. But some New Testament churches have had failure in their home mission work.

Even though we maintain a mother church is not necessary to authenticate a New Testament church, this is the way God usually works. It is usually best for one local church to start another one. Nature teaches us that like begats like, and vibrant New Testament churches begin similar churches. By this means the new congregation has the correct blueprint to insure success.

The church planter should not attempt to organize/charter his own church. He should invite his home pastor

Notes

or the pastor of a recognized church in the area. Since chartering/organizing involves recognition, he should attempt to get a church that is well accepted and that has the type of recognition that the church planter will want his church to have in the future. Also, an administrator from a Christian school could conduct the service for the church planter.

The author has organized churches during the Sunday morning service, the Sunday evening service, and on special meetings held during the week. The service usually includes singing of hymns, special music, preaching followed by the organizational/chartering service.

The sermon at an organizational/chartering service differs according to the leading of the Holy Spirit on different men of God. The author usually preaches on the nature of the New Testament church (see chapter 3).

I preached a sermon at the organizational meeting on the responsibilities of members of their church. Since the New Testament church was a group of baptized believers, I challenged them to faith in Jesus Christ and to receive only those into fellowship who had like faith and had been baptized. Since a New Testament church had the presence of Jesus Christ in their midst, I challenged them to allow Christ to shine through their corporate testimony and to use every means possible to hold forth the light of Christ into the city of Lincoln. Since the New Testament church placed itself under the discipline of the Word of God, I challenged them to reverence, believe, obey, and teach the Word of God. Since the New Testament church is organized for evangelism, education, worship and fellowship, I challenged them to give attention to their organization and always to keep soul-winning foremost in their program. Since a New Testament church administers the ordinances of baptism and the Lord's table, I challenged them to baptize all who came to know Jesus Christ and to administer the Lord's table to accomplish its purposes. Since the New Testament church is evidenced by the exercise of spiritual gifts, I challenged the congregation to follow the leadership of their pastor, a gifted man.

At the end of the sermon the author reads the statement of incorporation (see Appendix). This is a historic statement that has been used to charter Baptist churches for many years. First, he reads the statements of Baptist polity. As each statement is read, the congregation is told that they must

give adherence to their position if they will be a
New Testament church.

> 1. The pre-eminence of Christ as our Divine Lord and Master
> 2. The supreme authority of the Bible and its sufficiency as our only rule of faith and practice
> 3. The right of private interpretation and the competency of the individual soul in direct approach to God
> 4. The absolute separation of Church and State
> 5. The regenerate church membership
> 6. The beautiful symbolic ordinance of believer's baptism and the Lord's Supper in obedience to the command of Christ
> 7. The complete independence of the local church and its interdependence in associated fellowship with other churches
> 8. The solemn obligation of majority rule, guaranteeing equal rights to all and special privileges to none
> 9. A world-wide program of missionary fervor and evangelism in obedience to the final command of the Lord Jesus Christ
> 10. The personal, imminent, pre-millennial return of the Lord Jesus Christ.

Next the author points out that he does not give them spiritual recognition with God or with other churches. He explains that chartering/organization is similar to the ordination service. Both organization and chartering does not make the minister or church more Godly, nor does it endure them with power. Both recognize the work that God has done. Ordination is a service where the church recognizes that God has called a man to full time service. Chartering is a service where a congregation is acknowledged as being called together by God and is therefore given the authority that belongs to a church.

The author points out that the document begins "We the undersigned," hence placing the authority to organize on the people and not on the person who is conducting the service. Finally, the document concludes, "We assemble ourselves as _____ Baptist Church." In the final analysis, the church is the final authority. Therefore, the people organize themselves into a church. This action does not take away from God's authority, but enhances it for Christ indwells every believer, the Holy Spirit guides every believer and every believer is his

Notes

own priest to interpret Scripture; therefore, God establishes the new church through the medium of His people.

> Why Believers Are The Authority In The Church
>
> 1. Christ indwells each believer
> 2. Holy Spirit guides each believer
> 3. Each believer is responsible to interpret Scripture
> 4. The example of believers authority in New Testament churches
> 5. The believers are to judge false doctrine and sin in the church

After the document to charter the church is read and explained to the congregation, the author ask that the first few rows in the auditorium be cleared. Then he leads in singing the invitational hymn, "Just As I Am." Those who want to became charter members are then invited to come forward and present themselves as candidates as charter members in the new church. The author explains, "Just as the chu uses the hymn "Just as I Am' when people are brought into God's family, we use this hymn when this church is brought into existence." He also explains that this hymn is symbolic of the church's commitment to soul winning.

The author explains that charter members will be received in three ways; (1) By letter from a like-faith church, (2) By baptism, and (3) By statement of faith and restoration, the candidate having been baptized since he was saved.

The author usually explains that the prospective charter members are not required to have their church letters with them in the service. One of the first official acts the new church will do is to write and request letters of recommendation from the former churches of its new members.

The author explains that some are present who have been saved since the church planter has begun the work of evangelism in the area. These should come and present themselves as charter members with their willingness to be baptized when the church conducts its first baptismal service.

Those who come forward to present themselves as charter members are then asked the following questions:

1. Have you personally received Jesus Christ as your Saviour and are you attempting to live for Him?

(Each prospective member answers, I have.)

2. Are you in agreement with the doctrines of this church and will you submit to the ministry of this church?

(Each prospective member answers, I will.)

3. Do you believe God has brought this church together, and will you commit yourself to its prosperity?

(Each prospective member answers, I do.)

The author then pronounces, "Since each of you has received Jesus Christ as your Saviour, and since each of you are in agreement with the printed doctrines that should be believed by a church, and since each of you believe that God is leading their church into existence and since you have pledged yourself to make this church a success, I recognize you as a New Testament church in God's sight."

The charter members should then sign the charter. Some new churches have individual sheets printed and the person reads the charter and signs it. Other churches have the charter printed on a large parchment and each new member sign the charter. It is then framed and posted in the church as a reminder of its heritage. The author usually encourages the church to have extra copies of the charter available for the members to keep.

After the charter is signed, the author reads the names of each individual charter member and announces that they are the charter members and he usually gives the total number of names. Then he announces the church needs to conduct a business meeting and describes the following items.

```
AGENDA FOR THE FIRST BUSINESS MEETING
1. Elect a church clerk
2. Adopt the name
3. Call the pastor
4. Receive the financial records
5. Discuss deacons
6. Vote to keep the charter open
7. Authorize a building fund
```

First, the author calls the meeting to order and elects a church clerk. The church planter usually has asked a qualified person to allow his name to be nominated. Usually the one suggested by the church planter is elected, but the process recognizes the authority of the congregation to choose their own church clerk.

Even though the church has a name, the "rubber stamp" by the congregation is a symbolic act that it have the final authority.

Notes

The church planter is technically the human founder of the church, but the church is now given the opportunity to call its pastor. They always call the one who was used by God to call it into existence. This vote reminds the pastor that the people have the final authority over the position of pastor in the church and that God gives him the office by his people. The church planter is reminded that he is both leader and servant. He leads the church, but always by their will and authority. It also reminds the pastor that God speaks through the voice of His people that He calls into His church.

The church should vote to receive the financial records of the young congregation. Actually all the gifts to the church before it was chartered will then be technically recognized by the IRS for tax deductible purposes. The church does not vote to approve the financial records that have been previously spent. The congregation should not be asked to do that because they have not seen the records. But all that the church planter has received and spend becomes a part of the first years records and will be audited at the end of the first year. When the church planter knows he must give an account for all finances, he will have confidence in raising money for the new church and will have accountability in all his expenditures.

The new church should vote to postpone the election of deacons for one year. The author warns a new congregation not to place men in that office even if they have previously served as deacons and are presently qualified. He challenges the men to earn the right to be a deacon by their faithful service to the church. The author has witnessed several deacon boards in new churches have tried to assume the control of the church. The author has given the following reasons why a new church should wait for one year to elect deacons.

WHY WAIT TO ELECT DEACONS

1. The church in Jerusalem waited approximately one year before electing deacons in Acts 6.
2. "Lay hands suddenly on no man" means a person should prove himself.
3. Every man in a new church can act as deacon for the first year.

The author suggests the pastor call all the men in the new church together when he needs deacons and let them act as a body. If a man has a gift of serving, he will not mind waiting and will manifest it by doing the work of a deacon with the other men of the church. Then as "cream rises to the top" at the end of a year, it will be evident to the church who should be the new deacons.

The church should vote to keep its charter open for a period of time. The names of charter members will be posted in the church and they will be given special recognition as those who sacrificed to get the church going. Perhaps, even in heaven, God will have special recognition for those who were responsible for getting local churches going. But there will be some who might not be present in the chartering service, but they will work just as diligently for the success of the church and should be recognized. Perhaps they were working, sick, or not even saved until the third or fourth Sunday after the chartering service. A vote should be taken to leave the charter open for 30 to 90 days to recognize others as charter members who will sacrifice just as much.

The final action of the chartering service is the authorization of a building fund. The author explains that the new church will be considered a "gypsy" in town until it gets property and constructs a building. Therefore he takes an offering in pledges and cash for the building fund. He challenges everyone to give, not just the charter members. He announces, "Just as we bring a gift to a new baby in the hospital, so we should bring a gift to this new baby church."

The church planter should announce the building fund for several weeks, before the chartering service. This can be a time of great rejoicing for the new church to reach a financial goal and experience victory.

Finally, the author challenges the new pastor to faithfully discharge his responsibility, even in discouraging times. Then, he gives him the promise of God and applied it to the congregation: "Faithful is he that calleth you, who also will do it" (1 Thess. 5:23). The promise of God is clear. If God has called this congregation together, he will perform its growth and ministry through pastor and people." The church planter is now the pastor. He is introduced to the congregation and given an opportunity to challenge his new church.

Usually, a reception with refreshments is held.

Questions For Review

1. Dallas Billington started churches through tent revival meetings. True False

2. The church is incorporated during the chartering service. True False

3. Landmarkism is the view that a church must have authority from the denomination before it can administer the ordinances. True False

4. The strongest biblical argument supporting a landmark view of church planting is found in the origin of the Samaritan church. True False

5. An organizational service simply witnesses to the fact God has organized a church. True False

6. It is usually best for one local church to start another one. True False

7. The pastor of an Independent Baptist church should organize the church himself to avoid denominational ties. True False

8. The author usually preaches on the nature of the church at organizational meetings. True False

9. Ordination is a service where the church recognizes that God has called a man to full-time service. True False

10. The final authority in the church is the pastor because he is God's man. True False

11. The church should not be named until the congregation can choose a name at the chartering service. True False

12. The church should technically call the pastor during the charter service. True False

13. The church should elect deacons at the chartering service because they are officers in the church and the church should have its embryonic organizational structure. True False

14. The church should receive an offering for the building fund at the charter service. True False

CHAPTER 6

BIBLICAL ANSWERS TO QUESTIONS ABOUT
CHURCH PLANTING

There are several questions regarding beginning a new church which require more than procedural answers. These are doctrinal issues that give direction to a young man starting a church. Even though the questions are organizational, there is a biblical answer to them.

1. <u>Who Can Begin a Church?</u> The question is occasionally asked, "What agent/agency does God use to constitute a local church?" Some feel that only one New Testament church can constitute another church. They feel this way because of their doctrine of baptism--every person must be baptized by a person who has been properly immersed. They trace their authority to baptism back to John the Baptist. Its adherents believe a new group of people cannot begin administering baptism or the Lord's table until they get authority by being organized from a duly constituted New Testament church. It is a question of successionism.

There are problems with this view. First, the argument becomes continuous in time, and every local church must trace the authority of its baptism back past the mother church to the grandparent church to the great-grandparent church *ad infinitum*. The author believes that when a local congregation meets God's requirement, they become a church. Then they can baptize with the authority of Christ, not the authority of the mother church.

The second argument against successionism is the church in Samaria. Philip went to Samaria and preached the gospel, baptizing them (Acts 8:12-17), before the Jerusalem church sent Peter and John down to determine the Samarian church's credibility. Also, the church at Antioch was apparently organized and responsible for a great revival long before the mother church at Jerusalem put its stamp of approval on the new congregation (Acts 11:21-24). So, new churches in the Scriptures began without the vote of approval from another congregation.

Third, Jesus is the agent that founds the church. He called it "my church," meaning a congregation belongs to him. Also, he states, "I will build," indicating that a group of people must be put together by Jesus Christ to qualify for being a local church. The word for church, *Ecclesia*, means "to call out." Jesus calls men to salvation and places them in his body, the church. This is how he builds the church. Christ is the architect, designer, contractor and, finally, he occupies the church. "And hath put all things under His (Christ) feet, and gave

Notes

Him to be the head over all things to the church, which is the body" (Eph. 1:22-23). Christ also fills the church with his light (John 8:12); hence, it is called a candlestick. Obviously, Christ fills the church with his fulness causing us to say the church is equivalent to Jesus Christ, from beginning to end. Just as the body belongs to the head, Christ is the head of each local body. When Christ does the work, it is the church. Therefore, the organizational meeting is just "recognition day." As the author said at one service, "We're just watching what God is doing. My organizational powers won't make this church any more spiritual...any more powerful...it won't even make this congregation an authentic church. If God has called you together, this congregation is now a church."

Fourth, many young men have gone out from fundamental colleges and started a successful New Testament church. These men were not commissioned by a New Testament church. They just went out to begin a church in obedience to the call of God, relying on the power of God, building on the Word of God. True, they have been ordained by a New Testament church and sponsored in college by that church. When they went to a new community, their home church considered them "their boy." However, there was no official commissioning service to set them aside for starting the new church. This does not mean the new congregation lacks any spiritual power because there was no official vote by the mother church. Gerald Fleming graduated from Baptist Bible Seminary, Fort Worth and went to Dayton, Ohio, struggling for weeks before a group of people began meeting regularly. Bruce Cummings also graduated from Baptist Bible Seminary, knowing he wanted to start a church somewhere in Ohio or West Virginia. God led him to Massillon, Ohio, and a church of 2,000 evolved; once again, without a sponsoring church.

Other New Testament churches grew out of existing congregations and at a time in their existence, became a church. Curtis Hutson was a part-time postman and pastor in Decatur, Georgia when he read in a discarded issue of The Sword of the Lord that Dr. Jack Hyles baptized over 2,000 converts in one year. Thinking the statistic was a mistake, Hutson went to hear Hyles speak. While listening to Hyles give his famous lecture on soulwinning, Hutson realized two things. First, he determined his was not a church. He determined to go back and preach the Word according to the commandments of Jesus Christ. Second, Hutson determined that he could win souls. The following Saturday, he led three people to Jesus Christ. There was not a week since that time that Hutson did not lead someone to Jesus Christ at Forrest Hills Baptist Church. The church became a true New Testament church without the sponsorship of another congregation.

Fifth, some New Testament churches have started a mission congregation which failed. If there was any magical success to rub off from the mother church, insuring the existence of its children, surely the new church would have had it. But some New Testament churches have had failure in their home mission work.

Even though sponsorship by a mother church is not necessary to authenticate the new church, this is the way God usually works. It is usually best for one local church to start another. Nature teaches us that like begats like, and vibrant New Testament churches produce similar churches. By this means the new congregation has the correct blueprint to insure success.

Jesus Christ uses human instruments to establish new churches. The church at Samaria was begun by Philip. He preached (Acts 8:5), won souls (Acts 8:6), and they were baptized (Acts 8:12). Since baptism has a twofold meaning: (1) personal testimony, and (2) being added to the church, Philip must have realized the church in Samaria had been brought into existence. The church at Antioch sent out Barnabus and Saul to start churches (Acts 13:1,2). One of the criteria for a New Testament church is the evidence of spiritual gifts and leadership (Eph. 3:7-12).

Many young men have gone out from Liberty schools and the Baptist Bible College, Springfield, Missouri and started successful churches. Their success is not that they were sponsored by a mother church (many of them were not). Rather, their success came from the spiritual motivation they received from their college and home church. They were taught correct doctrine and correct methods. Because they followed God's pattern, he blessed their efforts and used them to build great New Testament churches.

Not everyone can begin a church. A man must be called into full-time service. This call involves a burden to win souls, a desire to preach and a compulsion that a man cannot do anything else in life. A man must surrender to this "call" and prepare himself accordingly. When he is ordained, it is an outward recognition that he is called by God. Then God leads that man to a community to begin a church. Or in some cases, a group of lay people have a burden to start a church. After they pray, God leads a man to them to establish a church.

2. <u>Should a Man Begin a Church in His Home Town?</u> Many young men have gone back to their home towns and started churches. In so doing, they have followed the example of several pastors of growing churches.

Notes

```
┌─────────────────────────────────────────────────┐
│      SUCCESSFUL HOME TOWN CHURCH-PLANTERS       │
│   Jerry Falwell        Lynchburg, Virginia      │
│   Harold Henniger      Canton, Ohio             │
│   Carl Godwin          Lincoln, Nebraska        │
│   Lamarr Mooneyham     Durham, North Carolina   │
└─────────────────────────────────────────────────┘
```

There are several advantages in returning home to begin a church. It is an area where the church-planter: (1) knows his way around, (2) has many friends, (3) already has a natural love and burden, (4) understands the community background and culture, and (5) would naturally remain a long time, giving opportunity to build a stable work without being called to another location. A great number of men in America return to their boyhood home to either become pastor of an established church ot to begin a new one. Perhaps these men are reacting to the American mobility--we are a rootless sociey in a floating world. They have a natural desire to settle down and build a stable church. When a young man looks around for a permanent neighborhood, the most natural place is back home.

```
┌─────────────────────────────────────────────────┐
│   ADVANTAGES OF RETURNING HOME TO PLANT A CHURCH│
│   1. Natural love and burden for community.     │
│   2. Understanding of the "life" of the community.│
│   3. Knowledge of the community (roads, services, insti-│
│      tutions, etc.).                            │
│   4. Established friendships and contacts.      │
│   5. Natural tendency for stability.            │
└─────────────────────────────────────────────────┘
```

However, one abstacle a young man faces in returning home is found in the exhortation, "A prophet hath no honor in his own country," (John 4:44). Some quote this verse to prove a preacher should leave his home town and go minister elsewhere. This appears to be a natural explanation. However, a close inspection of the verse and context reveals otherwise.

First, Jesus returned and ministered to his own area even though they did not believe him. The unbelief of the people limited his "mighty works" but did not prevent them (Matt. 13:58).

Second, the verse says nothing about successful ministry in his home town; it indicates only that he is "without honor." A pastor does not need honor in the community to be successful. He will be honored by his church. He must have the power of God upon his life and follow the guidelines of the New Testament.

Third, other biblical spokesmen went back to their own people, such as Paul who was ministering in Tarsus when Barnabas called him (Acts 11:25). The Old Testament prophets preached to their own people, as did Jesus' disciples (Mark 2:21-31, 2:1-12).

      After writing the book, <u>The Ten Largest Sunday Schools</u>, the author noted that those who built the largest churches settled down in one location for a lifetime ministry. For the past few years, he has urged young men to settle down and invest their life in one community, building a strong New Testament church. Out of this urging some young men have returned home to build a church. This raises the question, "How does God lay a city upon a young man's heart?" and "How does God lead a minister to a city?" Sometimes the natural love a man has for a city can be used of God to become a supernatural call.

      3. <u>How Shall Finances Be Given To Help a New Church Get Started?</u> At times, the more help that is given to a new church, the less it seems to grow. Like children, it is possible to do too much for them and spoil them. The Grant Memorial Baptist Church of Winnipeg, Canada had five mission works in outlying communities during the '60's. None of these works became a church even though the mother church did much for them.

      On the other hand, some mission churches die because they do not get needed help. Bill Monroe had started Florence Baptist Temple, South Caroline and was selling products door to door to make a living. The church was struggling financially as was Monroe. The Bible Baptist Church of Savannah, Georgia began sending $100 a week. "I worked more enthusiastically than ever," testified the energetic pastor. The church thrived. Four years later, they had an auditorium that seats 1,200 with an average attendance in Sunday School of over 900.

      The young church needs help, but what kind and how much? First, financial support can help its growth. Some want to give a weekly stipend or the gift of land. Maybe the very young congregation would prosper if it had the down payment on its first building, either as a gift or as a loan. But a warning is necessary. This type of money can hurt rather than help. A large Presbyterian church established several mission churches, but the Board of Elders at the mother church insisted on control of the finances, approval of business, and appointment of all new pastors. The people in the mission congregation did not feel the obligation of the ministry; therefore, they never supported it with their service or gifts. The missions all eventually died. Be careful of gifts from one church to another. The indigeneous principle demands that a church should be "self supporting." Therefore, it is better to give to support the church planter. Let

Notes

his work build the church and let the church raise money for its land and building. The Liberty Baptist Fellowship and Baptist Bible Fellowship follow the principle of supporting the man, rather than supporting projects in the new church.

> Financially support the church planter.
>
> Then let him build the church with finances from the congregation.

Dallas Billington began a number of churches throughout Ohio from his pastorate at the Akron Baptist Temple, the largest Sunday School in America at the time. For some of these churches, he donated hymnbooks, renting buildings for others. His main contribution was leading a revival in which the new church was born. Billington's status as a church leader, along with his ability to win souls, launched the new church with a better opportunity for success, than if the pastor had begun on his own.

An established church can supply workers to help get a new church started. These can be soul-winners, bus workers, musicians or teachers loaned on a temporary basis. At other times families can be sent permanently to help establish a new work.

An established church should not consider itself too small to help a new work get started. The Rincon Baptist Temple, Rincon, Georgia sent its Wednesday prayer meeting offering to a new work in Metter, Georgia. At the monthly meeting of pastors in the Baptist Bible Fellowship, new works are encouraged. Each month, testimonies of pastors in new churches are given. Some large churches contribute directly to the new church (not going through a central treasurer). But most amazing of all is the struggling churches that give sacrificially to the pastors of churches weaker than themselves.

4. <u>Shall the New Church Be Called Baptist</u>? There are some young men who think it is easier to plant a new church if it does not have the name Baptists. They want to call it "community," "Bible," or "Congregational." If these men think that people will attend if the name Baptist is not there, they are mistaken. The title "Community" or "Bible" or other non-offensive names have no meaning to the community. The church planter is saying his new church will not take a stand on the vital issues.

Some young men say that the name Baptist has a "bad" name in the community. Dr. Falwell says, "Then determine to make the word Baptist a good name."

Other young men think they will start with a

neutral name and change it later. Again, Dr. Falwell notes, "They won't change, it is easier to start right, than to try and make a church right at a later time."

There are five reasons why a church should have the name Baptist.

a. <u>The name Baptist says the church carries out the Great Commission</u>. The purpose of the church is to complete the command of Christ to go win lost people, baptize them and teach them. When a church carries the name Baptist, it tells the community that the most important function is the initiatory rite of water baptism after a convert is saved.

Since a name ought to point out the most outstanding characteristic, the name Baptist says that soul winning is more important than lituragy, education or fellowship.

Also, since a name should separate and eliminate confusion, then the name Baptist will separate a church and its soul winning function from other churches in the community that have compromised their stand on the gospel.

b. <u>The name Baptist says a church is committed to doctrine</u>. Baptist churches are usually committed to the essentials of Christianity. However, in our day there are some Baptist churches that have become liberal. But even so, when a church is identified by water baptism, it is taking a stand on the death, burial and resurrection of Jesus Christ. A church that is baptizing new converts is reaffirming its commitment to the lost condition of men and the results of sin which is Hell. It reaffirms these doctrines because it is trying to keep sinners from going there. The church is also reaffirming its commitment to the substitutory blood atonement. Most liberal Baptist churches have outwardly denied the doctrines behind water baptism because they do not baptize people getting saved. They usually just baptize children growing up in the church.

Also, when a church uses the title Baptist, it is telling the community it believes in eternal security. The last part of baptism is identification with Christ's resurrection. The resurrection of Christ gives eternal life and that lasts forever. Because the Free Will Baptist deny eternal security, many independent Baptists will not accept their members by transfer of letter.

c. <u>The name Baptist says a church is committed to New Testament church polity</u>. The name Baptist reflects

Notes

congregational authority, that in the final analysis the people are the final word. The pastor is the leader of the church and in most Baptist churches, he is the moderator of business meeting (which is biblical), while the deacons fulfill the meaning of the Greek word for deacon--they serve the church.

d. <u>The task of baptizing came from heaven</u>. It was pointed out to John the Baptist that Jesus was baptizing more than he was. In most cases this would be a blow to a man's ego to lose his influence with the multitudes. But John the Baptist answered, "A man can receive nothing, except it be given him from heaven" (Jn. 3:27). Here John was explaining that he was baptizing because it was a command from heaven.

When Christ gave the Great Commission to go and preach, he added "baptizing them in the name of the father, and of the son, and of the Holy Spirit" (Matt. 28:19).

e. <u>The name Baptist means acceptance by the people</u>. A Baptist church is usually a church of the people. Baptist churches are found among the poor and rich, among the educated and untaught, among all ethnic groups and in every part of the world.

In some locations the name Baptist has been tarnished by a church split or an ecclesiastical dictator. In other places the name Baptist has been associated with heresy or liberalism. But these are usually the exception rather than the rule. Since the name Baptist has been used for biblical reasons, the church planter should use it. In the last analysis, the people will support the church if the power of God is there and if the church is biblical. They will not care what others have done under the Baptist label. The people will support a church because of what it is doing, not because of its name.

5. <u>Should a Church Planter Work to Support Himself?</u> This is a question of "tentmaking." It is generally agreed that the apostle Paul worked as a tent maker in Corinth with Aquila and Priscilla (Acts 18:3). Authorities recognize that all Jewish boys were taught a trade, a man who was a rabbi as was Paul, was not omitted. The question arises, why did Paul work?

On the surface, the work of Paul could have been a stumbling block. Leon Morris writes, "The Greeks despised all manual labor, thinking of it as fit only for slaves."*

---

*Leon Morris, <u>Corinthians</u> (Grand Rapids: Wm. B. Eerdmans Publishing Company, 1958), p. 81.

But the answer goes deeper and is found in the indigeneous nature of the church. In Acts 20:24 Paul testifies that his own hands ministered to his necessities. In another place he reminds the Corinthians when he made tents, "And labor, working with our own hands" (1 Cor. 4:12). He continues in this verse to describe tent making "being reviled, we bless; being persecuted, we suffer it." Apparently, Paul was criticized for tent making, but continued his labor. Also, Paul tells the Thessalonians, "For ye remember, brethren, our labor and travail; for laboring night and day, because we would not be chargeable unto any of you, we preached unto you the gospel of God" (1 Thess. 2:9). The word for labor is "kopiomen" which means hard work to the point of being uneasy. Again Paul notes, "Neither did we eat any man's bread for nought; but wrought with labor and travail night and day, that we might not be chargeable to any of you" (2 Thess. 3:8). Paul's reason for working was to remove any criticism regarding his motives for preaching the gospel. But there could also be a second reason for tent making, any support he took for the new church might have weakened it's growth. And finally a third reason for Paul's work was to be an example to the Greeks that God expects a Christian to earn his food by the "sweat of his brow." The Greeks in certain cities were not industrious, and because of this Paul only worked in certain cities. In other places he was supported by outside finances (Phil. 4:16).

When a modern church planter earns his living, (1) he is self sufficient in his ministry. Too many church planters let their families bear the sacrifice alone of building the new church. (2) The church planter meets people while employed who are prospects for his church. (3) He also knows the pressure of his people and can better minister to their needs. (4) The church planter becomes a testimony to the people of the church for them to be diligent employees. (5) Working will give the church planter many opportunities to share the gospel with the lost. (6) Finally, the church can never accuse the church planter of being lazy and when he is finally supported fulltime, they will have confidence in the work he does at the church.

But there are implied dangers to "tent making" by the church planter. (1) The church planter will have less time to pray, read and prepare his messages. The church planter must grow if he expects the church to grow. (2) He will have little time to visit or give counsel to needy individuals. (3) Concentration will be a third problem. How can he fully give himself to his work (which he must do as a conscientious Christian) and fully fully give himself to planting a new church? Even if he can do both, what about his family responsibilities?

(4) The working church planter may hinder the church because it takes away from its indigeneous nature. A church should be self-supporting, but the working church planter is supporting the church. By his example, the church planter is telling his flock they do not have a financial obligation to support him. (5) The last drawback to tentmaking is that it is a possible hinderance to faith. Instead of trusting God to supply the needs, the church planter is trusting his ability to make money.

In the final analysis, many church planters will have to work to get started. The many church planters who have worked to get their church started should be applauded. On the other hand, just as many church planters have had their needs met and they never had to go into the secular job market. They should praise God. God has used both methods to get a church started and the potential church planter will need wisdom to find God's plan to support his new church.

Questions for Review

1. Baptist get their name from John the Baptist who started the first Baptist church.	True False
2. A new church may baptize converts without the authority of a mother church.	True False
3. Philip's ministry in Samaria and Gaza is a strong argument for successionism.	True False
4. The charter service marks the church becoming the body of Christ.	True False
5. New churches are truly started when sponsored by large churches.	True False
6. Graduates of BBF schools start many churches without the sponsorship of a mother church.	True False
7. The easiest place to build a great church is in your home town.	True False
8. Home town pastors tend to remain longer in their pulpit.	True False
9. Home town pastors may be reacting against U.S. mobility.	True False
10. A pastor cannot be successful without the honor of the people of the community.	True False

11. God may use a man's natural love for a city to call him there to start a church. True False

12. Churches should not support new churches because it weakens them. True False

13. The church planter will work harder and preach better if financial support is kept to a minimum. True False

14. Money given for church planting should be designated to support the pastor, not church projects. True False

15. A church should not begin to get involved in church planting until membership reaches 100. True False

16. More people will attend a new community church than a new Baptist church. True False

17. A wise pastor will not call his church Baptist if the name has a bad reputation in the town. True False

18. The name Baptist identifies the church with the work of the Great Commission. True False

19. Even though some Baptists are liberal, the name Baptist communicates to most people certain doctrinal commitments. True False

20. The rite of baptism originated on the day of Pentecost. True False

21. Baptist churches reach people across various socio-economic lives. True False

22. The Greek word for labor ($\kappa о\pi \iota о \mu \epsilon \nu$) means to reproduce your ministry in the life of a disciple. True False

23. According to the Scripture, Paul made tents in Corinth, Ephesus, Antioch, and Thessalonica. True False

24. Tent making is the best way to finance a new church because it takes financial pressures off new Christians. True False

SECTION II

SIX METHODS OF CHURCH PLANTING

There are at least five different ways to plant a church, plus one that we believe to be the most influential. There is more than one method to plant a church. Neighborhoods are different (inner city, rural, racially mixed, upper class, etc.), people are different (spiritually mature, uneducated, rebellious, etc.) and the church planter has different strengths (evangelistic, Bible teacher, counselor, musical). Hence, there seems to be different strategies to start a church. All of them will work under some circumstances, but the sixth method is the one recommended at Liberty Baptist Schools.

First, some recommend the mother-church concept, whereby one congregation breaks off part of its members and sends them to another section of town, and constitutes them into a New Testament church (Chapter 7).

A second method plants churches by first establishing a mission Sunday school. When it has sufficiently grown, it becomes a New Testament church. Dr. Lee Roberson Highland Park Baptist Church in Chattanooga, Tennessee, established over 13 churches in his area through this method, plus he has over 100 mission Sunday schools most of which are pastored by the students of Tennessee Temple University (Chapter 8).

A Bible study group is the third method of beginning a church. As people study the Word and are nurtured in the Scriptures, they sense a growing burden to organize into a New Testament church. Whereas this method has not been used among Independent Baptists, it has been used by the Bible church movement and other groups such as the Evangelical Free Church of America (Chapter 9).

The fourth method is church planting through the local association, as advocated by the Southern Baptists (Chapter 10). The fifth method is planting new congregations through church splits. Sometimes Independent Baptists laugh about church splits, and other times we cry over them. Nevertheless, God has used it as an effective method of reaching people for Christ (Chapter 11).

The sixth method is the pioneer church-planter going into an area to plant a New Testament church (Chapter 12). Independent Baptists are known for their "hot poker" philosophy of leadership, whereas the success of a church depends upon the stature and influence of its pastor. Hence, the founding of new churches depends upon the church planter.

CHAPTER 7

MOTHER-DAUGHTER CHURCH PLANTING

When the author organizes a new church, he normally gives the new congregation several prayer goals. One challenge is that God would call some young man in the new church to enter the ministry. This is in keeping with God's plan of reproduction. In the first chapter of Genesis we read that plants and animals reproduced after their kind, each producing its unique fruit. Fruit bearing is a universal principle. The fruit of an oak tree is the acorn which gives birth to another oak. The fruit of a peach tree is a peach with its seed which, will produce another peach tree.

There is a technique of church planting that grows out of this principle, it is each church producing another one just as a mother gives birth to a child, so a mother church gives birth to a new church.

Timothy Starr, home missions secretary of the Fellowship of Evangelical Baptist Churches in Canada, urges churches in his group to take a more active part in church planting by this method. This is accomplished when the mother church commissions several families to start a new "daughter" church, usually in an area nearby that needs evangelizing. When Doug Blair moved to Sarnia, Ontario to begin the Bluewater Baptist Church, several families from the larger Grace Baptist Church formed the nucleus of the group. Also, Blair was able to have an office in the mother church and was paid a full salary by the mother church as a staff member. The combined assets of the mother church helped the new church get started. This strategy was also used in the new Erin Mills community in Mississauga, Ontario. Erin Mills Baptist Church began when several families from Kenmuir Baptist Church in Port Credit were sent out to start the new congregation. The original group included a Bible College teacher who gave leadership to the group until a pastor was called. In contrast, when Wishingwell Acres Baptist Church in Toronto, Ontario learned that Thorald Marsaw was planning to pioneer a new church in North Toronto, he was invited to meet with several church families who lived in that area. Instead of being a pioneer church planter (see Chapter 12), he lead the new church in a mother-daughter relationship. The successes of these and other new churches started this way has resulted in church growth among Fellowship Baptists in Canada.

The first step to starting a church this way is taken by the mother church. A survey of church families is done to determine where clusters of families may live.

Notes

Next, a survey is done to determine the needy area for a new church. In connection with this survey, possible meeting places and church sites are also considered. Timothy Starr advises that a report be made to the mother church and that a vote be taken to approve the action.

The strength of mothering a new church is that the outreach comes from the Christians of a church. After all, they are the church and when they are willing to sacrifice themselves for the new church, it will have a better opportunity for success. The weakness is the lack of a man (church planter) who has the vision and burden to go to an area to bring the new church into being.

The group that goes out from the mother church would normally include a cross section of the church's membership. If mature Christians remain in the mother church, the new church will struggle with leadership if it depends on those won to Christ in the new area. On the other hand, if too many mature Christians leave, it could hinder the continued ministry of the mother church.

The new church group will keep their membership in the mother church until the new church is chartered. This way they have all the advantages of church membership (Lord's Table, etc.). When people are saved in the new church, they become a member of the mother church until the members are officially broken off into the daughter church. This sometimes solves the problem of people who are reluctant to join a new church for its lack of stability and permanence.

Starr claims this method of church planting not only reaches the new area, it also serves to revive the mother church and train its members. Most mother churches testify that the space left by those who go to the daughter church is soon filled by new members. Thus two churches experience the benefits of this method and no one loses.

Immanuel Baptist Church, Ft. Wayne, Indiana planted several churches throughout the area by this method. When Immanuel was averaging 400 in attendance, the author preached on the Sunday when a group of its members chartered the Black Hawk Baptist Church. In 1981 Black Hawk was averaging approximately 1500 in attendance, attesting to the practicality of mother-daughter church.

George Bell, home missions representative for the Fellowship Baptist in Ontario, advises pastors that starting daughter churches should be a part of the long range plan for every church's evangelism and missions program. With this in mind, the area in which new churches are to be planted can be prepared for several years before. A church may conduct a Vacation Bible School or operate a Sunday School bus in the area. Also, Christians in the area may be organized for home Bible studies and/or prayer meetings.

Several churches in the decaying inner city have moved to the suburbs by this method. Instead of moving in one giant leap, the old church began a daughter church in a new area. Gradually, as the members moved to the suburbs, the daughter church got stronger. The pastor of the mother church alternated his preaching schedule to minister with more frequency to the daughter church. The mother church took on more ethnic/social ministry to those in its changing neighborhood. While this illustration is not the same as reaching a new area by church planting, it follows many of the same principles.

There are several problems confronting this method of church planting, most of which relate to the mother church. While most churches will agree to start a church in two or three years, they are sometimes reluctant to give up tithing members when the specific starting date arrives. Also, some churches are unwilling to give their assets to the infant congregation. A third problem with the mother church is provincialism. Many churches fail to see the need in their own town. They may give thousands of dollars to missions in foreign countries but fail to see the need to start a church on the otherside of town. They may argue that the mother church would remain empty if several families started a new church but normally the reverse is true. Both churches experience growth in attendance almost immediately.

A final problem involves the mentality of certain big churches. The mother church thinks it can better minister to the people with better preaching, music, programs, service, etc. The larger church wants to continue to grow and see the daughter church as a threat to its progress.

This plan of church planting is achieving results in many established cities. These are successful among those who will not attend the fundamentalist store front mission in the poor part of town. Also, these churches are able to achieve a degree of financial stability after erecting attractive buildings within a few years. In large cities where land and building prices prohibit the building of a large campus ministry or a multicultural neighborhood hinders the growth of the church, the objectives of the church may be best accomplished through daughter churches. While pastoring Oakwood Baptist Church in Toronto, George Bell led the church to begin a Filipino speaking Baptist church in the same neighborhood. Cultural differences made it difficult to reach Filipinos

Notes

in the English church and their population in Toronto warranted starting the new church. Many city churches have begun ethnic daughter churches giving the daughter church use of their facilities for a Sunday afternoon service until the new church can build or buy their own facilities.

Questions for Review

1. A mature church will always start a new church.   True   False

2. Daughter churches are started when several families leave a church over a doctrinal issue.   True   False

3. Mother-daughter church planting is most effective in rural areas because farmers travel a long distance to town.   True   False

4. Those not actively involved in the ministry of the mother church are the best prospects for a new church.   True   False

5. A church survey should indicate where clusters of families live and areas that need a new church.   True   False

6. Daughter churches can never be started off bus routes.   True   False

7. The mother church can sponsor home Bible studies and vacation Bible schools to prepare for a new church.   True   False

8. It takes two to three years for the mother church to recover what is lost to a daughter church.   True   False

9. Provincialism is a problem that keeps a mother church from planting a daughter church.   True   False

10. Many churches are reluctant to send out members to start a new church for several reasons.   True   False

11. Ethnic churches can rarely use the facilities of a white English speaking mother church because of racial prejudices.   True   False

12. This method of church planting never involves a church planter but always relies on the members of the mother church.   True   False

13. Daughter churches tend to be reflective of the strengths and weaknesses of mother churches. True False

14. This method of church planting is being used by super aggressive large churches that are growth oriented. True False

15. The very nature of daughter churches make them pastor led in administrative leadership. True False

CHAPTER 8

MISSION SUNDAY SCHOOL CHURCH PLANTING

Using a mission Sunday School to plant a church is not a new technique. Actually, over 61,000 Sunday Schools were established by Sunday School missionaries employed by the American Sunday School Union between 1829 and 1879 in a campaign called the Mississippi Valley Enterprise. Many of these Sunday Schools evolved into Methodist churches because of their evangelistic fire that was covering the nation. A Sunday School mission is usually an evangelistic outreach where children and adults are brought together to be taught the Word of God in a systematic manner. The Sunday School mission is usually staffed by Christians from a nearby church and the expenses (rent, printed materials, travel, etc.) is paid by the sponsoring church. If and when property is purchased, it is owned by the sponsoring church. The difference between a mission Sunday School and mothering a new church is that the mission Sunday School was not begun with the purpose of being an independent church.

When the author was preparing the manuscript for The Ten Largest Sunday Schools he visited Highland Park Baptist Church in Chattanooga, Tennessee. On that particular Sunday in 1969, the local newspaper had an article in the feature section on 13 churches that had been planted by Highland Park Baptist Church. These churches had been planted through a mission Sunday School. At the same time the church has approximately 100 chapel/mission Sunday Schools that will never become autonomous local churches. In some the population is too small to support a church. In other areas, the population is to transient or too economically poor, or too uneducated. The people in the area need ministry, but there is not enough stability to support a church with its obligation to support a pastor.

Dr. Bill Monroe, pastor of Florence (S.C.) Baptist Temple has begun an evening Bible Institute with a view of training laymen to serve in mission Sunday Schools. Monroe sees approximately 100 areas in the rural areas of his section of South Carolina that need evangelizing, but the area will not be able to support a church. He has a vision of starting 100 mission Sunday Schools.

Dr. John Rawlings, pastor Landmark Baptist Temple, Cincinnati, Ohio, has started eight satellite churches in areas where Sunday School buses used to run. The satellite churches are actually mission Sunday Schools except they include a preaching service where one of the staff members from the sponsoring church preaches.

Notes

Only time will tell if the mission Sunday Schools of Dr. Monroe or the satellite churches of Dr. Rawlings will become indigenous churches. The main point is that the communities are reached with the gospel. In some cases, a mission Sunday School will be more effective, while in other cases the area will be best served by a local church.

LOCAL CHURCH	MISSION SUNDAY SCHOOL
1. Self Supporting — Controls income & purchasing.	1. Depends on sponsoring church. Property owned by sponsoring church. Offerings go to central treasurer.
2. Self Propagating — Can reproduce itself.	2. Ministry is led by Christians from sponsoring church. Mission people help in ministry.
3. Self Governing — Able to direct itself and is not controlled by outside influence.	3. Decisions for ministry and organization made by sponsoring church.

The author pastored a mission Sunday School for the Scofield Memorial Church, Dallas, Texas, as he was attending seminary. The work was called Dennison Street Chapel when the people called him as pastor in 1955 (the sponsoring church pastor had to interview the author to approve his appointment). In the next three years, the author built the work large enough (from 25 to 125), and increased the offerings so the work was self supporting. He led the congregation to write a charter and by-laws, elect deacons and build an educational building. The name was changed to Faith Bible Church. There was apprehension and delay in turning the property over to the new church because the leadership at Scofield Memorial Church felt the new work was not mature enough.

Many churches are going to mission Sunday Schools instead of extensive bus routes. As busing has become expensive, workers also realize it is difficult to have a continuing influence on people who are transported a great distance from their neighborhood. At the same time, a mission Sunday School has a continuing influence in the neighborhood of the pupil and he is identified with a gospel assembly by the lost people in his community. There is more stability in a mission Sunday School than in a bus route. But, Sunday School busing cannot be ruled out. Those who are taken to a larger church will usually be exposed to better and more extensive ministry.

	Mission Sunday Schools
Advantages:	1. Stability through outside leadership. 2. Outside financing pays for what the mission could not otherwise afford. 3. Represents an effective tool to reach areas of city for church.
Disadvantages:	1. Members of mission often do not accept responsibility for the work. 2. Many missions never become churches. 3. The nature of a mission keeps it from becoming self supporting, self governing, and self propagating. 4. The mission is often run by a board not involved in the work.

Used by Dr. Lee Roberson (Highland Park Baptist Church) and other pastors with colleges and churches in large cities.

The author feels that extension works are a wave of the future and will be used by evangelistic churches that want to reach their Jerusalem and surrounding Judea for Christ. The name given these extension works is not as important as the principle of extending the outreach of one church into a large area of influence.

Names for Outreach Ministries

1. Extension
2. Satellite Churches
3. Chapels
4. Bible Studies/Classes
5. Missions
6. Cell Groups

Notes

There are several societal factors that will contribute to an even greater outreach of extension ministries. First, advanced principles of administration and supervision will make it possible for a large church to give better guidance and support to outlying groups. Second, improved promotion in areas of Christian radio programs, mailings, advertisements, printing, etc., will make it easier for the sponsoring church to communicate its "heart" and the direction for ministry to its outreach groups. Third, improved communication in telephone, mails, printings, etc., will give the sponsoring church the tools to give direction to its extension works. Fourth, improved transportation will provide cars, buses, roads and mass transit to get gospel teams out to the areas away from the sponsoring church and to bring the masses back for special meetings. Fifth, money is available to finance the teams and provide the facilities for outreach into surrounding communities. The sixth reason involves improved understanding of the role of church and enlightened techniques of how churches are getting the job done. When a pastor knows what others are doing and how they get it done, he will follow their example.

Pastors who want to build great super aggressive churches are finding that there appears to be natural plateaus beyond which the church will not grow. These pastors are using extension works to reach new areas, extend their influence and continue their growth.

Just as America's ten largest Sunday Schools have been on the experimental cutting edge of new innovations coming into Sunday Schools, the ten largest churches in the world are leading the way in reaching their areas through extension works.

THE TEN LARGEST CHURCHES IN THE WORLD

	CHURCH	CITY/COUNTRY	MEMBERSHIP	AUDITORIUM	TYPE OF GROUPS	NUMBER OF GROUPS	ASSOCIATION
1.	Full Gospel Central Church	Seoul, Korea	160,000+	8,000+	Home Cell Groups	13,000+	Assembly of God
2.	Jotabeche Church	Santiago Chili	80,000	16,000	Temples	59	Methodist/Pentecostal
3.	Congregaco Crista	Sao Paulo, Brazil	61,250	3,000	Mission Churches	261	Pentecostal/Brethren
4.	Highland Park Baptist Church	Chattanooga Tennessee	58,000+	7,000	Mission S. Schools	116	Independent Baptist
5.	First Baptist Church	Hammond, Indiana	58,000+	5,000	S.S. Bus Routes	250	Independent Baptist
6.	Yung Nak Presbyterian Ch.	Seoul, Korea	35,000	4,800	?	?	Presbyterian
7.	First Baptist Church	Dallas, Texas	21,500	2,400	Mission S. Schools	13	Southern Baptist
8.	Madureira Church	Rio de Janeiro Brazil	20,000	3,000	Mission Churches	20	Assembly of God
9.	Thomas Road Baptist Church	Lynchburg Virginia	19,000	3,700	Plant New Churches	171	Independent Baptist
10.	Akron Baptist Temple	Akron, Ohio	18,000	4,800	Plant New Churches	?	Independent Baptist

Notes

The Full Gospel Church in Seoul, Korea, has continued to grow through cell groups in the homes of its members. These groups are: (1) controlled by the pastor in content, organization, personnel, and location within the city, (2) evangelistic, educational and worship (tongues) followed by fellowship, (3) offerings are sent to the church, (4) divided for growth by the pastor, (5) no property or facilities are purchased, (6) attendance and participation at cell groups extends to members of other churches, (7) the average size of a cell is 30 to 40, although a few have 200 to 300 members.

The Jotabeche Church in Santiago, Chili, has reached out through 59 extension groups, called Temples; the main church downtown is called the Cathedral. (1) Each temple has individual membership, plus membership in the mother church. (2) Each temple has a building that is owned by the mother church. (3) Each temple has a pastor that is responsible to Vasquez, pastor at the mother church. (4) All offerings go to the mother church. (5) Some temples have 1200 in attendance; others are much smaller. (6) Every Christian from outlying temples attends the mother church once a month. (7) Approximately 10,000 are regular attenders only at the mother church. (8) Growth is through street meetings and personal soul winning. (9) Outlying temples are churches in function.

The Congregation of Christ in Sao Paulo, Brazil, is a functioning denomination of 5,000 churches; yet in each city there is one mother church, each with many extension churches. The Congregation of Christ in Sao Paulo had 61,250 members as of Easter 1981 in the mother church and 261 extension works in Sao Paulo. (1) Everyone is a member of the mother church and takes communion in the mother church or in one of the ten designated churches. (2) The mother church plans, contracts for, and owns each of the extension buildings. (3) The only paid employee is the treasurer who serves all 261 churches. (4) All elders (approximately 750 pastors) are volunteer workers, with approximately five in each of the 261 churches. (5) The mother church is the central distributor of Bibles, printing, used clothes, and building supplies. (6) They evangelize an area by planting new churches.

Highland Park Baptist Church in Chattanooga has over 100 Sunday School missions with the following characteristics. (1) Operated by staff and students of Tennessee Temple University. (2) All those baptized are members of the mother church. (3) Mission Sunday Schools usually include both teaching and preaching. (4) When property is purchased, it is owned by the mother church. (5) Many groups meet in rented facilities, while others meet in old church buildings that have been purchased. (6) Most missions minister to disadvantaged groups of people so there is no plan to charter them into indigenous churches.

The other American churches have Sunday School bus outreaches which have some of the characteristics of outreach groups, except that children are brought back to the mother church.

The question is raised about Baptist polity. Can one group of people that have assembled in the name of Christ, control another group of Christian people? Or to ask the question differently, "Are Sunday School missions biblical, especially if they are never intended to be a church?" Then the churches of South America raise a question. Can one church own the property and control the ministry of another group of Christians, especially when the group may have 1000 members? Can one gathered church be divided into several smaller gathered assemblies?

The church at Jerusalem began with 120 in the upper room (Acts 1:14) and later had approximately 5,000 men, plus wives and children. This amount continued to grow so that Josepheus estimates that half of Jerusalem became Christian (estimates of 100,000 believers). Common sense would tell you that they gathered in smaller groups for prayer (Acts 12), study and fellowship. They are called a multitude ($\pi\lambda\acute{\eta}\theta\text{ους}$) singular. Later they are discribed as multitudes ($\pi\lambda\acute{\eta}\theta\eta\varsigma$) plural. Perhaps they were divided into groups or multitudes for efficiency. Later we know of the existence of house churches (Philemon 1:2, Rom. 16:5). Perhaps these groups centered their assembly in certain houses in Jerusalem.

Some have taught that the two epistles to the Thessalonians were written to two different sections of the church in that city. Paul's habit was to go and preach in the synagogue. Some of the synagogues were Christianized and one church in Thessalonica was predominantly Gentile (Illustration, "churches of the Gentiles," Rom. 16:4) while the other epistle was written to a separate Christianized synagogue but more Jewish in nature. Hence, one church but two gatherings in one city.

When Paul wrote the epistle to the Romans, he addressed it "to all that be in Rome, beloved of God" (Rom. 1:7). He did not address it to the church at Rome, perhaps because there was more than one church, or several assemblies of one church. He greets Priscilla and Aquilla, noting "Likewise greet the church that is in their home" (Rom. 16:1). Later in the same chapter Paul notes "Salute them which are of Aristobulus' household" (Rom. 16:10) implying a church assembly could meet there. He implies the same again, "Greet them that be of the house-

Notes

hold of Narcissus, which are in the Lord" (Rom. 16:11).

Paul writes from Corinth but states, "The churches of Christ salute you" (Rom. 16:16), implying more than one assembly in Corinth.

The above Scripture is all tentative, hence it only prohibits us from absolutely ruling out that a church may have one entity but several locations in a city. Hence, the ministry of satellite churches or mission Sunday Schools may be biblical in nature. Whatever the final conclusion, each church should evangelize its Jerusalem and then its Judea. Since the Bible is not explicit, the church should be as innovative as possible while never going against Scripture.

Questions for Review

1. The Mississippi Valley Enterprise used mission Sunday Schools to start over a thousand Sunday Schools a year from 1829-1879. True False

2. Usually mission Sunday Schools are not started to be churches. True False

3. Highland Park Baptist Church in Chattanooga, Tennessee, started over 100 mission Sunday Schools, plus 13 other churches which were started from church splits. True False

4. Bill Monroe plans to reach 100 areas in South Carolina using his trained laymen to start mission Sunday Schools. True False

5. John Rawlings opposes the starting of satellite churches operated by a mother church because he believes Baptist churches should be independent and self-governing. True False

6. Some churches are establishing mission Sunday Schools to replace extensive bus ministries. True False

7. The author believes evangelistic churches of the future will probably use extension works more extensively. True False

		Notes	
8.	Improved promotion techniques will aid churches in the maintenance of mission Sunday Schools.	True	False
9.	Extension Sunday Schools are one means of overcoming the natural plateaus of church growth.	True	False
10.	America's ten largest Sunday Schools are leading the way by establishing numerous extension Sunday Schools.	True	False
11.	Mission churches are a comparatively new phenomena and represent a structure foreign to the New Testament.	True	False
12.	The New Testament pattern of the church demands one larger church reaching the entire city.	True	False
13.	There are texts which seem to indicate that the church had more than one central location in Rome, Thessalonica, Jerusalem and Corinth.	True	False

CHAPTER 9

BIBLE STUDY CHURCH PLANTING

Many new churches are started from a Bible study class. There are several ways the new church comes about. First, the church planter goes to an area and begins a Bible study in his home or a neutral location. His long range goal is to begin a church, but his immediate goal is to gather a nucleus of people, win them to the Lord and nurture them in the Word of God. In essence, the Bible study is a "half-way-house" to a church. When the Bible study is large enough, the church planter turns it into a church.

In the second case, a Bible study grows because it is meeting the needs of those who attend. Because of its natural attraction of people and ministry to them, they call a pastor when they are large enough. Unlike the first illustration, they never intended to be a church, but it just happened.

Some churches have strategically placed Bible study groups in certain neighborhoods to evangelize them. They were not begun by a church planter as in illustration one, nor are they intended to nurture Christians as in the second illustration. They are usually led by laymen with a strong evangelistic thrust. They are accompanied by visitation, prayer for specific lost people and an ultimate desire to get them into the main church.

David Seifert, pastor, Big Valley Grace Community Church has begun a number of evangelistic Bible studies on Sunday evening with a view of reaching people for Christ. As they grow in strength, Seifert plans to let them grow into chapels of his church. At that time the Bible study will have its completed ministry to its members.

There are some liabilities to beginning a church through a Bible study. Sometimes the church planter is so cautious that he trusts his "flesh" and is afraid to publicly commit himself to a new church. This lack of faith hinders the blessing of God. Also, the "first seed reference" principle determine that a church will grow as it was planted. If it is not planted with vision, it will not grow with vision. Also, the Great Commission implies that a church be planted, converts be baptized and then taught all things (Matt. 28:19,20). A Bible study usually teaches Bible content only, and neglects to teach the new convert the obligations of service in the church.

Notes

```
┌─────────────────────────────────────────────────┐
│              BIBLE STUDY GROUPS                 │
│                                                 │
│ Advantages:  1. Churches are started.           │
│              2. Converts are committed to the   │
│                 Bible.                          │
│              3. Trained leadership can be pro-  │
│                 duced for the new church by lay-│
│                 men who are involved in the Bible│
│                 study.                          │
│              4. Stability (financial and spiritual)│
│                 can be built into the church.   │
│              5. Cases of church failure are     │
│                 eliminated.                     │
│              6. No temporary meeting facilities │
│                 are needed as the Bible study   │
│                 meets in homes.                 │
├─────────────────────────────────────────────────┤
│ Disadvantages: 1. Slow process.                 │
│                2. Many Bible studies never become│
│                   churches.                     │
│                3. A certain lack of faith by the│
│                   leaders. They do not outwardly│
│                   commit themselves to start a  │
│                   church.                       │
│                4. Often Bible studies lack direction│
│                   and evolve into doctrinal error.│
│                5. People are attracted to a Bible│
│                   study because of a doctrinal  │
│                   tangent.                      │
├─────────────────────────────────────────────────┤
│ Used by Rev. David Seifert (Big Valley Grace Community│
│ Church) to start churches, also found in Bible  │
│ churches and evangelical denominations.         │
└─────────────────────────────────────────────────┘
```

The home Bible study group is a new phenomenon in our nation. Some of these are called "cell-groups," or "the living room church," or "the underground church." The home Bible study is an evangelistic technique that takes advantage of American desire for dialogue and sharing. In a society of anonymity, people desire to share their problems and insight regarding the Word of God. Some are brought to a knowledge of Jesus Christ; others strengthened in their Christian life.

When Royal Blue (a man's name) went to Redding, California in 1962, he found a group of Christians who were meeting for prayer and Bible study--a group honestly seeking to do God's will. He recognized immediately that here was a group of people who had faith in God and trusted God. The group called themselves the Community Bible Fellowship and were not a group of community disgruntles. Sherman Fulkerth, who was then Mayor of Redding, California was the man giving direction to this small group. Royal Blue had worked with the large First Baptist Church of Van Nuys, California as Youth Pastor.

Blue told the people when he came to Redding, "You haven't told the city anything by using the name Community Bible Fellowship." Blue also indicated that the Bible Fellowship had not established doctrine; therefore, there was no basis on which members could join the group, nor were the people obligated to the group. He said the name "Community Bible Fellowship" could be a conglomeration of a number of beliefs, and even people from cults could be involved. "I am a Baptist, and I believe in establishing churches," he told the people in the initial meeting. He commented that several from the Navigators had been involved in the prayer group, and he endorsed people getting into the Word, finding salvation and stablizing their lives. However, Blue noted, "We must do more than get *into* the Word, we must get *under* the Word, and let the Bible give direction both to us as individuals and to us as a group." He also encouraged the people to obey the Lord's command to baptize new converts by immersion and to celebrate the Lord's Supper.

Blue did not set a goal to build a large church, but testified, "I conceived of a group of people who wanted to witness and take the gospel to the entire city of Redding and to the regions of Northern California." Out of North Valley Baptist Church has come the direction that is being afforded to 16 smaller churches in the Northern California area, all growing and reaching souls for Christ.

By 1973, the North Valley Baptist Church had over 1,800 members, a Sunday morning attendance of over 1,300 worshippers, and a weekly offering of between $6,000 and $7,000. Their missionary budget called for $50,000. The church property is valued at over one million dollars, and it has a youth camp at one-half million dollars. God is using the members of this church to influence others of the Northern California area; something that just a Bible study group could never have accomplished.

Most Bible study groups lack three qualities that have excluded them from becoming an aggressive New Testament church.

1. <u>A Bible study group usually lacks a leader committed to founding a church.</u> The genius of a Bible study group is interaction, each man sharing his insight from the Bible. Discussion, not a sermon, is the catalyst that makes it successful. Sometimes, those in a Bible study group come from many churches; other times, group

Notes

members come from an unchruched background. Usually a dominate leader destroys the inherent nature of a Bible study.

 2. <u>A Bible study group lacks commitment to church ordinances.</u> The ordinances of Baptism and the Lord's Table belong to the local church. Individuals should not practice these ordinances, nor should a Bible study group until they are constituted as a New Testament church. Even though a pastor gathers people to study the Bible, they should not practice the ordinances apart from a New Testament church. When a group of Christians organize themselves according to the New Testament, they will want to obey the two commands: (1) "Go and make disciples...baptizing them" (Matt. 28:19), and (2) "Take eat, this is my body" (1 Cor. 11:23,24). Since these are commands of our Lord, the Christian who does not join himself to a church that observes the ordinances properly cannot be in the perfect will of God.

 3. <u>A Bible study group does not have an obligation to corporate ecclesia (the embryonic church) through mutual fellowship, attendance, financial support, and numerical growth.</u> Many attend a Bible study group because of the personal enrichment they receive. (This is an honest contribution to the cause of Christ.) However, the same Christians would have grown more spiritually if they had been members of a church where they accepted the obligations that would have developed them greater. When an individual accepts the obligation of membership in a New Testament church, he must financially support the group, understand its doctrine, support its services, and involve himself in Christian service through that church. An individual becomes a better Christian by placing himself under the discipline of a church.

Questions for Review

1. Bible study groups fulfill the Great Commission because they teach Bible content which will motivate Christians to win the lost.   True   False

2. A church can be started from a Bible study even when this is not the intention of the founding group.   True   False

3. Church planters should start using Bible studies to plant a church to save money on the renting of facilities.   True   False

4. Churches begun as Bible studies often reflect a lack of faith on the part of the church planter.   True   False

5. The popularity of home Bible studies is a result of the desire of many people to dialogue and share.   True   False

6. Churches differ from Bible study groups in terms of the aim of the group and their desire to obey Bible imperatives.   True   False

7. Churches started by Bible studies often attract a greater number of mature Christians committed to biblical doctrine.   True   False

8. An established church can use laymen to start new churches using this method.   True   False

9. Bible studies tend to develop the leadership skills of those in charge.   True   False

10. A Bible study started with a view to becoming a church should regularly participate in the Lord's Supper together.   True   False

CHAPTER 10

ASSOCIATIONAL EFFORTS TO PLANT A CHURCH

In recent years, many pastors have seen value in cooperating together to start new churches. To a greater or lesser degree one purpose of a denomination is for the purpose of church planting. In most established denominations, it is a matter of relying on the home missions department to provide leadership in church planting.

The impetus for church planting in most denominations does not originate through existing local churches but rather through central initiation. The members of the denomination's home missions committee usually represent ecclesiastical authority to plant new churches. In groups with a strong central authority such as some Presbyterians, groups, new churches are authorized by the denomination and/or synod, etc. Local churches are usually not encouraged or permitted to start new congregations.

While not organized as strongly, many independent Baptist have come together in state BBF meetings and groups like Liberty Baptist Fellowship for Church Planting. These fellowships differ from associations and denominations of churches in that they are a fellowship of pastors, rather than an association of churches. Whereas a denominational structure often results in a central authority that gives direction to local churches, the leadership of groups like L.B.F. are subject to the authority of Baptist pastors. Also, pastors' fellowships tend to avoid overhead expenses in the work of church planting. Denominations often hire staff and provide many services to help plant new churches, resulting in increased overhead expenses.

The work of church planting through associations cannot be overlooked. The Southern Baptist Convention starts over 500 churches per year. Other Baptist denominations also emphasize church planting as well as many non-Baptist groups. In many respects, there are assets to church planting by denominations. First, denominations maintain schools where men are trained in their distinctives resulting in increased personnel to pastor existing churches and plant new churches. Also, church loyalties to a denomination make raising money for church planting somewhat easier. Many groups have special funds to finance new churches at little or no interest. When a group of laymen desire to begin new church, they will often contact a denomination with which they are familiar thus

Notes

providing a loyal group for the church planter to build with. Also, many developers will negotiate church sites with major denominations before a community is planned resulting in ideal community sites for the new church.

Of course, there are some who oppose denominations and will not consider starting churches through associations. They point out that even in Baptist groups, the mission church rarely has complete autonomy. Often a pattern of control has been established in a church's history leaving some to wonder if the church is ever self-governing in the strictest sense of the word. This problem is further complicated if the new church receives financial aid on its first building.

Church associations tend to stress administrative efficiency over grass roots participation. While a denomination attempts good stewardship of resources, a resultant side effect is often a decreased zeal and vision by the church. The independent pastor must depend upon the Lord to meet his needs whereas the denominational pastor always has an alternative source.

Most denominations have a regular strategy by which they start their churches. Of course, every church is different, but the general principles usually apply. Southern Baptist writer Jack Redford suggests nine steps in planting a new church. When a denomination begins an outreach in a new town or section of a city, these steps provide the general guidelines they follow. In some cases the order of these steps may alter but this is the exception rather than the rule.

NINE STEPS IN CHURCH PLANTING*

1. Select a missions committee
2. Select an area for a new work
3. Prepare a sponsoring church
4. Cultivate the field
5. Begin a mission fellowship
6. Organize a mission chapel
7. Finance the work
8. Provide facilities
9. Constitute the church

---

*Jack Redford, Planting New Churches (Nashville, Tennessee: Broadman Press, 1978), pp. 27-108.

If an association of churches were to start a church in Virginia, the first thing they would bring a group of people together to give guidance for the new church. Most denominations have a standing committee for this purpose. After surveying the area, they would choose a place to begin the church. When the area was chosen, churches in that association would be contacted to consider sponsoring the new church. This idea of sponsoring a church is similar to the idea of daughter churches and mission churches.

The next major step is cultivating the field. Floyd Tidsworth* suggests there are many ways a new area can be prepared for a new church. One church hired a college student to conduct a recreation program in town. Other churches have conducted Vacation Bible Schools or operated bus routes in the area. Pastor Wally Mills organized a Sunday School for six months before holding the first service of Current River Baptist Church in Thunderbay, Ontario. The media has also been used effectively to prepare the town. Some writers call this preevangelism.

The growth of the new church occurs in three phases. First, the mission fellowship is established. This will usually take on the form of a home Bible study or cottage prayer meetings. As an interested group is gathered a missionary chapel is formed. The members of this chapter will be the charter members of the church. At this point the church planter will raise money for the new church from sponsoring churches and the denomination. Also, he will secure facilities for the new church to hold services. Plans will be made for the church to enter its third phase when the chapel is constituted into a church. Many denominational leaders suggest a recognition council be called so that area churches affiliated with the denomination will be able to share in the organizing of a new church.

---

*Jack Redford, Planting New Churches (Nashville, Tennessee: Broadman Press, 1978), pp. 27-108.

Notes

ASSOCIATIONAL EFFORTS
Advantages: 1. A planned strategy to start churches. 2. Utilization of the assets of many churches to begin a new church. 3. Administrative Efficiency over other methods of church planting. 4. Room for grass roots participation. 5. Denominational loyalty of pastors who are willing to support a new church in their state/province.
Disadvantages: 1. Pastor/Planter limited in decision making authority. 2. God uses men not committees to get His work done. 3. There is a question if God intended for denominations to exist. 4. Limited in evangelistic vision and the purpose of a church.

Questions For Review

1. Liberty Baptist Fellowship for church planting is an association of Baptist churches committed to church planting. — True False

2. The central authority in most denominations are the pastors of local churches. — True False

3. Denominational overhead costs are higher because of services offered to churches. — True False

4. Fewer new churches are started by established denominations than are started by independent churches. — True False

5. Denominations are an asset to church planting in the area of financing new works. — True False

6. Denominational identification will help the church planter gather a solid and unified group to begin a new church. — True False

7. Major land developers are prepared to plan new communities in consultation with denominational leaders regarding religious institutional designations in a city plan. — True False

8. The church planter can affiliate with a denomination and start a self-governing church if he affiliates with a Baptist denomination. — True False

9. Denomination church planting capitalizes on grass-roots participation because everyone can give to the home missions fund. — True False

10. Churches cooperating in associations to start churches are usually motivated to do so to achieve good stewardship of resources. — True False

11. The financial support from an association of churches normally swells the church planter's vision and zeal. — True False

12. Because every church is different, there can be no basic strategy to church planting. — True False

13. Most denominations have established mission committees. — True False

14. Preevangelism is expressed by the phrase "cultivating the field." — True False

15. A denominational church cannot be organized without a recognition council. — True False

CHAPTER 11

PLANTING A CHURCH FROM A CHURCH SPLIT

Many new churches are started from a church split. As obnoxious as a church split may appear, there are times when God leads a group of people to leave their church and plant a new one. There are certain advantages and disadvantages in beginning a new church with a group of people who have left another church.

Planting Churches From Church Splits	
Advantages:	1. Churches have financial commitment. 2. New church has a core of people. 3. New church has committed and mature Christians. 4. New group is closely knit around a cause.
Disadvantages:	1. Usually poor reputation in the community and among other Christians. 2. Bitterness may hinder its ministry. 3. New church may be established from some other reason than evangelism. 4. People who could not get along with others in the old church will cause problems in the new church. 5. Strong opposition from old church.
Used by fundamentalists with liberal churches and charismatics in non-pentecostal denominations.	

The attitude prevalent in the Christian world is that a church should never split. Since Jesus said, "I will build my church" (Matt. 16:18), most think it is presumptuous to "split" a church that Christ built. It is difficult to analyze issues that lead to a church split, because splits are usually born of emotions rather than rationality. Good men have deep feelings concerning church splits.

Those who feel a church should never divide usually question any group splitting a New Testament church. The motives of any pastor who has successfully led a split are doubted. The idea of a church split is rejected even though

Notes

there is some validity to this position. Some will split a church over the smallest issue. Some, like spoiled children, will pick up their toys and go elsewhere to play (lead a fraction out of a church). A few pastors who receive a majority vote may try to "run out" those who voted against them. When people leave a church individually, this is known as splintering a church.

Church splits have their humorous side. When interviewing a pastor of a large northern church, I asked how many churches he had started. "Several...but none by design," he replied. Another pastor stated, "We've had so many splinterings that we have supplied kindling wood leading to revival fires all over the city."

Is there a proper way to split a congregation, bringing glory to God? Some say no! At the same time, fights, arguments, court cases, name calling, ugly scenes and adverse news coverage cannot help the cause of Christ. Paul and Barnabas had been a successful missionary team, planting churches. The two men had been friends since Barnabas had befriended Paul immediately after his salvation, when no one else would. These men were closer than any pastor and staff member. Yet, when approaching their second missionary journey, Barnabas wanted to take young John Mark along. Paul objected. "The contention was so sharp between them, that they departed asunder from one another" (Acts 15:39). God used Paul's temper to double the missionary endeavor, and two teams went out instead of one.

In one sense, most American churches come from a split. A new church in an old neighborhood is established from the same motivations that a split occurs; i.e., the old churches are not getting the job done. However, young churches in new neighborhoods are usually established out of evangelistic endeavor. There were many churches in Roanoke, Virginia, but Rudy Holland established Berean Baptist Church.

Some leave denominational churches to start churches, splintering their efforts because they feel their denomination is dying. Since individuals do not come as a unit, they cannot be called a church split. Yet families were dissatisfied with their home churches. Over 200 people left the Highlawn Baptist Church in Huntington, West Virginia to begin the Fellowship Baptist Church. They came as a unit. Some of these had been in the previous church all their lives. Their time, money and prayers helped build their church, yet they left it behind. Usually when one family leaves an old dying church to join a young vibrant congregation, other families follow. Like the first trickle of rain cutting a ravine through newly plowed dirt, the stream grows wider.

Most church splits arise over personality rather than doctrine. Individuals could not get along. Two good friends can disagree over an issue but love each other in the Lord. They remain friends, yet the same issue would split those who already have a basic dislike for each other.

In spite of all the unfortunate church splits, God has used many to his glory. People have been brought to salvation who would not have otherwise been reached. Communities have been evangelized, colleges built, missionaries sent out, and money raised that would never have come from a complacent, dead church. God causes even the wrath of man to praise his name (Gen. 50:20).

When Should a Split Occur?

The one basis over which churches should split is the candlestick (Rev. 1:19, 2:1,5). When a church is in danger of losing its existence, it should take measures that will return the candlestick to its original brilliance. (The candlestick is Christ, the Light of the World, dwelling in every believer as he joins in corporate assembly to evangelize the community.) Since the church is a unity, the responsibility of the church rests upon every member. It is the duty of the whole church to: (1) preserve unity, (2) maintain correct doctrine, (3) practice pure living, (4) elect leaders to carry out the church's purpose, and (5) exercise discipline. Each member is responsible to make sure the candlestick burns brightly. When it does not, they should take biblical steps to put the church in order. If they cannot correct the problem, should they stay and submit, or leave? When God removes his blessing from a church, it is time for the zealous believer to leave. As a result, a church split is not just a terrible appendage in the program of God; it is the final step when a church has lost its candlestick, or the church's existence is threatened.

1. <u>A church split is justified if the church is not baptizing new believers</u>. If new converts are not being baptized, the church is not winning souls. Therefore, the "candlestick" is in jeopardy and flickers low. This may be a basis for a group of people to leave a church and start another one. Some maintain Christians ought to remain and serve the Lord in a dead church because they can win souls and influence a few people in their Sunday School classes. However, a layman can only do so much. The pastoral and board leadership will inevitably influence the church according to their objectives. If they are not winning souls now, there is little possibility they will do so in the future. If Christians leave and join a vibrant New Testament church, they will accomplish much more with the same energy in the new church than in the former dead church.

Usually, people remain in dead churches because of friends or the church buildings and equipment. The freedom of serving

Christ in a biblical church has greater rewards, even when the facilities are less than adequate. A church is not the building or its facilities. There is a question whether faithful Christians can get control of the church property and assets when they are the minority. They can claim to be the true church because they are faithful to New Testament doctrine. But if they do not have the majority, it is best to leave; they have no other alternative.

2. <u>A church split is justified when doctrine is compromised.</u> The New Testament church was bound together in stability by the harmony of its doctrine. Even at the Jerusalem Council, when they disagreed over doctrine, the churches were strong enough to override the schismatic nature of divided opinion. Church splitting over doctrine is seldom a black-white issue; there are shadows of gray that cloud the issue. When a group of people in a liberal church find Christ as Saviour, those controlling the church are not hospitable to fundamental doctrine. It is easy to see how disagreement over doctrine would cause these Christians to break off into a new church. However, a congregation is the body of Christ. A body usually grows cohesively as a unit. Therefore, if the whole church is growing in knowledge and faith, there should be no disagreement of doctrine. The people should grow together in understanding. The church should have harmony of doctrine. Yet, individual Christians will never find another person with whom they completely agree. Therefore, there will be disagreements within a church. Church splits are justified because of disagreements over major issues of doctrine, such as the virgin birth, the inspiration of Scripture or the nature of baptism. However, should churches split when they disagree over the nature of man: i.e., one Christian feels man has a dichotomous nature, while the second believer feels man has a body, soul and spirit?

Pure doctrine is not the ultimate or only purpose of a church; it is the means to an end. The objective of a church is the Great Commission. But correct doctrine is the only foundation on which evangelism and the Christian life prosper. The Bible is the foundation of the church, and no local church could be built without correct adherence to doctrine. However, when a cohesive group of people are held together only by pure doctrine, they tend to major on minor variations of dead orthodoxy, leading to sterile sermons. In turn, this may lead to unjustified church splits.

A church may compromise its doctrine and conscience by continued affiliation with a dying denomination or affiliation with unscriptural organizations. A church may compromise its doctrine by allowing outside speakers who hold an unscriptural stand. Doctrinal compromise makes it impossible for a church to fulfill its obligation to the

Scriptures and carry out evangelism; therefore, a group of people have a Scriptural basis to form a new church. This should be done only when it can demonstrate that the present church has broken fidelity with the New Testament.

3. <u>Impurity is another factor that can lead to a church split</u>. A local church, like individual Christians, should live holy lives a part from sin. Just as God will not hold the Christian blameless who sins, so God demands purity in the church. When a church permits obvious sin to persist in the congregation with no attempt to correct it, the blessing of God will be taken from that church. However, a split is justified only when sin keeps a church from fulfilling its basic purpose in life. The following cautions are in order: (1) Every church has some evil present for no man lives without sin. Therefore, no group of people is completely pure. (2) If a church is attempting to deal with its sin, a young hothead should not try to split the church. (3) There will usually exist sin in fringe members. This is not a basis for a church split. A split is justified when there is obvious compromise in the pastor, deacons, or workers.

Impurity that leads to a split may grow in two areas. First, a church allows public sin to remain in its leadership. This might be in its board members, teaching staff or pastor. These men may have unconscious sins which are not obvious to others. These will not necessarily hinder the testimony in the community. A congregation must work, pray and encourage one another in this cause. The second is public sin that destroys the church. Those who want to remain pure should try to exercise church discipline. When it fails, they are free to establish a new church.

The author believes a fundamental church recently lost its candlestick when the pastor, an evident preacher of the Scriptures, divorced his wife. The candlestick could have remained if the people had voted to remove its pastor, but they did not. Both people and pastor are living contrary to the New Testament. Can God bless this church with his presence? When Christians find themselves in a church that will live contrary to the New Testament, they should split and join/form another church.

Attitudes During Church Splits

The following attitudes can help bring glory to God in the middle of a split. Recently a denominational official said to the author, "You fundamentalists are always splitting churches. We liberals never split a church." His remarks put me on the defensive. We fundamentalists seem like underdogs who take our toys

Notes

and go home (start over again) when we can not get our way. But liberals do not give attention to biblical doctrine, pure life or winning souls. Since they did not have an objective position to hold, they could drift with any current. Therefore, they would not fight, nor do they have the strength of commitment to start over again; i.e., to split and begin a new church. The following principles will help guide those caught up in a church split.

1. <u>Keep issues centered on doctrine, not personalities</u>. Ever since the author was a freshman in college, he was heard it said that a church split centers on people, not doctrine. There is no statistic to verify this conclusion, but it probably reflects most church splits. People get mad at the preacher and look for an issue to justify their leaving to start a new church. At other times, two factions within a congregation oppose each other. Often, when there is a doctrinal issue, it is obscurred by personal feelings. Some issues are brought to congregational vote, just to "straighten" out other people in the church. When a church faces a split, examine the issues to determine if doctrine or personality is the key issue.

2. <u>The motive to start a new church should be to fulfill the Great Commission</u>. Often, a new church is started just to get away from corruption or to find a new base for fellowship. The desire for separation from doctrinal corruption is commendable but is not a sufficient basis to start a church. Some have left a church that is squabbling, seeking peace in a new church. As much as church fights are deplored, harmony is not the ultimate purpose of founding a new congregation. A church is organized to carry out the Great Commission. Even if the new church has fundamental doctrine, it will not prosper as God wants it to prosper unless soul-winners will evangelize the neighborhood.

3. <u>A church split should follow the scriptural pattern of dealing with grievances</u>. First, when a man has a charge in his heart against a brother, he should face him with the issue. Second, the Scriptures indicate that the offended should take someone else with him when airing his grievance. Finally, the issue should be brought before the church. Here the constitution and bylaws of the church should be followed and the grievances brought out into the open. No church split should be attempted before first bringing the issue to the church as a whole. Discuss it--rationally. Ask for people to examine Scripture and pray over the matter. Then, if nothing can be resolved, the parties who start a new church will have no guilt feelings. They have proceeded according to Scripture.

4. <u>Keep all motives pure</u>. When Christians disagree it is easy for jealousy, strife or spite to influence their feelings. Keep a sweet spirit. When Abraham's herdsmen had a disagreement

with Lot, they reminded themselves, "We be brethren" (Gen. 13:8). When you disagree with other Christians, remember, they are born again by the same blood. If the church is apostate, you are not dealing with Christians; they are lost people. You have an obligation to live before them as before heathen.

5. <u>Do not win the battle and lose the war.</u> Some church splits have been so "hateful" that both sides destroy their reputation in their city. After the severance has been made, they are not able to win lost people to Christ because of their unchristian spirit. Therefore, judge every action by the "long look." The new church will have to live in the community. When a new church is born in friction, it usually "fights for its life." Beware of getting the reputation of being contentious and antagonistic. This is the wrong image for a church. Of course, you will "contend for the faith," and you will "resist the devil." Make sure the community knows why you fight. A church should be militant, but at the same time it must be loving.

This chapter does not encourage church splits, but recognizes their inevitability. The author's prayer to the Lord is, "That they may be one" (John 17:11). However, because sin infiltrates the church, because men are drawn away into false doctrine, because Christians tend to grow cold in their love and because churches die, church splits are inevitable. My advice to those who split churches comes from a package of dynamite I once saw when an uncle was blasting stumps: "If you do not know what you are doing, do not touch. If you do--handle with care."

Questions for Review

1. Church splits should not be encouraged because it is always better for a church to resolve its problems and grow in that experience.   True   False

2. An analysis of church splits demonstrates most splits occur over doctrinal error or immorality in the church.   True   False

3. Splitting a church occurs when factions develop within the church and begin lobbying their special interests.   True   False

4. According to Acts 15, Paul and Barnabas split over the circumcision of Gentiles.   True   False

5. Most American churches come from a split. True False

6. The responsibility for church unity rests only with the pastor because everything rises or falls on leadership. True False

7. Churches should split over doctrine because pure doctrine is an ultimate purpose of the church. True False

8. Doctrinal compromise makes it impossible for a church to fulfill its obligation to the Scriptures and carry out evangelism. True False

9. Church splits are characteristics of fundamentalism. True False

10. The chief motive in splitting a church and starting a new church should be doctrinal purity. True False

11. The Bible presents a plan of church discipline to follow before splitting a church. True False

12. A church should be militant and loving. True False

CHAPTER 12

THE PIONEERING CHURCH PLANTER

The sixth method of church planting is the pioneering method used by many young men in independent fundamental churches who go to the city for which they have a burden and do everything within their ability to get one started. They do not wait for a church to evolve out of a Bible study nor do they work through a Sunday School mission. They do not split a church nor do they use a group of people from a mother church to start a new church. They go because there is a need i.e. there is no soul winning church and there is a great number of unevangelized people. The pioneer church planter makes things happen because he is an innovator and a change-agent. He makes the circumstances that gives birth to the new church. He does not make a new church happen, for only Christ can do that. But the church planter knows the spiritual dynamics that are necessary to plant a church and he lets Christ plant the church through him.

1. <u>The personality trait of the church-planter.</u>

Some often ask if there is a personality type that is more successful in starting churches. Some think the church-planter must be the rugged individualist who can persevere in spite of the odds. Others think he must be a charismatic personality attracting poeple to himself, hence building the church on his own charm. From the author's observation, he has seen all types of men build churches. Bill Monroe who founded the Florence Baptist Temple was shy in meeting people, yet aggressive in doing the work of God; so was Carl Godwin in Lincoln, Nebraska. Rudy Holland is the unstoppable force who can plow through the immovable object--with love. The builder of churches in rural areas with dogged determination, attracts the rugged farmer.

Since Jesus is the founder of the church, he uses human channels who are dedicated to him. Only God can accentuate a man's talents, while at the same time compensating his weaknesses. God uses the inadequate individual with meager abilities and marginal equipment to serve in limited circumstances. When he is God's man, he beats insurmountable odds, overcoming oppressive obstacles to accomplish a work of God. Never was this more demonstrated than in the men who are planting churches.

Men who start churches must be pioneers, and only certain men have that trait. These men must be willing to swing a hammer and negotiate a loan. They must promote in the pulpit and advertise in the newspaper. They must preach, counsel, rebuke and teach the Bible. A pioneer must be able to do it all, for he usually begins with little if any help. The pioneer must lead people to Christ, nurture them in the Scriptures, train them in service and inspire them to spiritual greatness.

Some church pioneers go from one challenge to another. They have ruggedness to "plant" but lack the patience to "water" (1 Cor. 3:6). Praise God for church-planters. Missionary Lonnie Smith in Monterrey, Mexico has planted over 50 churches. Praise God for pastors who build. Dallas Billington did both, founding the Akron Baptist Temple and building it to over 6,000 in Sunday School.

The man who would begin a church must be *humble*, realizing that it is God who works through all of his abilities no matter how strong or lacking. He must have vision as the prophet of the Old Testament called a *seer*, (1 Sam. 9:9) because he was the eyes for God--seeing first, seeing farthest, and seeing the most. The man who would start a church must by faith see the church completed in his heart before a soul is won or a brick is laid on the foundation. *Courage* is another attribute of the church-planter, he must face discouragement and disappointment. Some of those he leads to Christ will turn their backs on the Lord. Other young babes in Christ will not grow according to his expectations. No congregation will grow as rapidly as the pastor expects, nor will the new building be as elaborate as the pastor desires. He needs courage to accept the present without letting discouragement rob his future. *Compassion* is another needed quality. Who can build a church without the love of God flowing through him? The church-planter must love people, want to be with them and desire to serve them. *Tenacity* is needed in every successful life. The church-planter cannot build a church without persevering; he must never give up. A new church is an endless struggle. Because he senses God's call to a community, he does not turn back because of opposition. Because he has a burden from God for a city, he rejects calls to settled pastorates and established salaries. "Jesus steadfastly set his face to go to Jerusalem," (Luke 9:51) where he would die for his people. The church-planter must have the same determination. He will build a church because he made a promise to God and to himself.

The church-planter must embody all the qualities of the Christian life because, as the shepherd of the flock, he is their example. Being controlled by the Spirit in his preaching, teaching, soul-winning and church management is only the first step. The church-planter must display the fruit of the Spirit in his personal life so that others desire to be like him. If the list of qualities for a church-planter were complete, it would be as long as the requirements for any pastor. To make the qualifications short and understandable, he must simply be "God's man" in the community, doing what Christ would do.

2. <u>The management style of the church-planter.</u>

The church-planter is like the self-made businessman. They are the rugged individualists. However, with time, they change their role and self perception. As others with the gifts of leadership arise in the congregation, the role of pastor-pioneers have changed. They must share their work with deacons; they work through superintendents, and they work within the organization they have built. They build organizational structure, giving away some of the authority that was theirs without losing the influence of their leadership.

When discussing a change in pioneer-pastors, it is really growth we are describing. The man who has a long successful pastorate is a growing Christian. He must grow in status as his church grows in size and influence. His capacity, ability and compassion must grow as the problems of a larger congregation become more complex.

In the military, the role of leadership changes. The lieutenant who leads an attack up a hill becomes the general who plans strategy behind the lines. The pastor who lays concrete block with his men becomes the manager of a multi-million dollar corporation. What was once a high-structural management changes to a shared-management concept of leadership.

The field of management recognizes the need of a strong personality at the inception of a business. Called high-structural management, or downward cycle, the entrepreneur or businessman is the pioneer, personnel manager, visiting fireman and motivator all wrapped up in one man. The aims, motivations and evaluations reside in the man. The owner and the business are inseparable; he is the company. Usually, the employees work for the boss and have a direct relationship with him.

After the company has existed for a length of time and has grown large, new needs arise that demand a different kind of management. Employees lose contact with the boss, and bureaucracy settles over the organization with its accompanying apathy and sometimes atrophy. Shared-management, goal-setting and an upward cycle of change is necessary for business prosperity.

After a new business is started and a new manager moves into an existing industry, he uses a low structured

Notes

management (the typical American church). This leader attempts to introduce change from the bottom. With this method, a training program communicates new knowledge which is supposed to change the attitudes of the employees, thus modifying individual behavior, ultimately changing group behavior. This is the upward cycle of leadership where management is shared with employees following the route of "indigenous leadership." The employee is given reasons, motivation, and training to improve his task in the company. As he improves, of course, production improves and profits rise. This is often called an upward cycle in management to curb deteriorating employee-employer relationships. The result is improved esprit de corps among the entire business.

The high-structured management begins at the top and forces coerced change downward through the system. The manager sets standards for the entire group which may be in regard to goals of production, codes of dress, regulations concerning behavior, etc. The theory of high-structured management is: (1) group behavior is the result of individual conformity to group standards; (2) individual behavior is slowly internalized; (3) the individual begins to assume the attitudes of the corporation and those who work around him. Finally, he takes on (4) the knowledge he needs to improve himself and ultimately the company.

When a pastor takes over a church in existence, he usually must use low-structured management or plan change to make upward improvement in the organization. This involves leadership training classes and education, the upward cycle having a leavening effect on the entire church. Sometimes, a young man comes into an old church with great zeal, yet lacking knowledge and uses a high-structured management trying to enforce group behavior on all church members. This usually results in (1) a split congregation, (2) the loss of certain members, or (3) the firing of the pastor.

The young man who begins the church must begin with a high-structured leadership because there is no existing organization. There must be a downward cycle because he usually personifies the standards of behavior and service in the church. The new church does not have group behavior, so it must be set by the pioneer-pastor. Dr. David Staffer of Calvary Christian Temple, St. Louis, Missouri justified, "I had a new church with unstructured Christians. I could not let them determine the standards of the church, so I had to crack the whip with love." Staffer, who understands business management, indicates, "I enforced a coercive style of management realizing I was causing a volatile reaction among some people, but there was no other way to get the church started." Staffer ultimately wants to reverse the cycle of planned change from a downward cycle to an upward cycle in management.

3. The church planter faces insurmountable odds with limited resources in unlikely circumstances.

The man who desires to build a church is usually motivated by the "impossible dream" and he must accomplish the "unperformable task." A church is never a human invention nor is it a man's accomplishment. An *ecclesia* is a people "called out" from sin, beckoned to gather themselves in God's assembly. They are "called out" from normal pursuits to carry out God's commission. The church is established by God, is empowered by God and, ultimately, God is its objective. Those who would start a true church must be motivated by God who is its founder.

The world does not love a church because it convicts the surrounding community by its purity and humility. The world still hates Christian influence. It will not embrace a new church nor will a community naturally support a beginning church. God must perform a miracle each time a new church comes into existence.

Into this improbably situation steps a man. As once "There was a man sent from God whose name was John," (John 1:6), just so God always has a man who will step into the gap (Ezek. 22:30) and respond, "Here am I, send me" (Isa. 6:8).

When the human race was threatened by sexual abuses, God worked through his man--Noah. When the nations were given over to idolatry, God had his man--Abraham. When the world faced seven hard years of famine, God had his man--Joseph. When the people of God were groaning under an oppressive slavery in Egypt, God had his man--Moses. God's man always attempts the unattainable, whether his name is Samuel, David, Nehemiah or Paul.

God still uses a man. One of the greatest tasks a man can do today is start a church. A man begins by obeying God's call. Next he faces his "unattainable task" and in the power of Christ accomplishes a victory a mere individual could never win. He influences his neighborhood, yet must do so in the spirit of humility. He does not desire self-popularization. It is God he magnifies. But when he has successfully accomplished his goal of starting a church, he is both well known and influential. Yet notoriety must never go to his head; to remain influential he must remain humble.

A church is always built *by* a man, but is never built *on* a man. Churches started by committees never seem to prosper. God's grace and power must be poured into a man--God's servant. Remember, "A great church is always *caused*, it never just happens." God always has his servant who sacrifices, prays and works.

Notes

James Mastin who drove into Milwaukee with all his furniture loaded on a U-Haul truck appeared about as formidable as David standing before Goliath with five stones. But God still uses the unaided man with limited resources against insurmountable obstacles in unlikely circumstances. Mastin knew no one in the city, had little finances and faced deep religious conviction. Yet, God used James Mastin to plant Central Baptist Church.

Although God does not use a modern Gideon to slay an army of Midianites with 300 faithful soldiers, he still uses the same principle. God still uses the unaided man as he used Moses against Egypt, Samson against the Philistines and Joseph to feed a famine-infested world.

Dr. G. B. Vick, Pastor of Temple Baptist Church, Detroit, has said, "Great men build great churches while average men serve average churches." If a young man wants to start a church that will be influential, he must study great men. A pastor becomes like the minister he patterns himself after. Some mission churches fail or stagnate because their leaders lack well-balanced spiritual leadership. Simply, the church fails because the leader has not learned the basic steps of Christianity.

To build a great church, a man must have developed a stern hard-headed tenacity. "I'll never give up," Rudy Holland affirmed, banging his fist into the palm of his hand. But the church planter must also nurture the devotional meekness of Puritans. He must have physical endurance not to crack when his young converts deny the faith. The pastor-leader must have a reverent sense of spiritual things, yet the cold calculating eye of a businessman. He must be quick to acquire knowledge in a thousand areas where he is ignorant, yet must lead authoritatively for no one else in his congregation knows how to build a church. The pastor-founder must speak persuasively in public and listen sympathetically in private counsel. The man who would establish a church must be an extraordinarily equipped man of deep commitment, iron will, wide scholarship and unblemished experience. If he does not have it all when he begins, he must gain it soon and in the acquiring process he will build a church. If he does not personally grow in ratio commensurate to his vision, he will never establish and build the great influential church of his dreams.

As Daniel stood before the lions...

As David slew his ten thousands...

As Elijah stood alone on Mount Carmel...

Today, young men still go forth to establish a church...

	Pioneer Method
Strengths:	1. Churches are started. 2. Pastor/Planter has greatest liberty in guiding a church into the New Testament model. 3. Church is as strong as the ability of the pastor to produce growth. 4. Fit the role of the New Testament church planter.
Weaknesses:	1. The church will reflect the weaknesses of the pastor/planter. 2. The motives of the pastor/planter may be suspect. 3. Pastor must work or arrange outside financing. 4. Extreme pressure on pastor/planter and his family.
Used by Liberty Baptist Fellowship for Church Planting and many Independent Baptist who start churches after graduating from schools like Baptist Bible College, Hyles-Anderson College, etc.	

Questions for Review

1. The pioneer church planter does not wait for a church to evolve out of a Bible study or Sunday School mission but rather makes the church happen from the start. | True False

2. To pioneer a new church the pastor must be a rugged individualist who has the personality to plow through problems. | True False

3. God uses different kinds of men to pioneer a church. | True False

4. Because the pioneer church planter must do everything at the start, he must be an experienced pastor. | True False

5. God uses some men to start churches and leave the church to plant a second church, rather than stay and build a great church. | True False

6. The church planter cannot build a church without persevering. | True False

7. The pioneer will avoid experiencing discouragement through careful preplanning. | True False

8. At the start, the church planter must be evangelistic rather than emphasizing Bible teaching in his preaching. | True False

9. The qualifications for the church planter are the qualifications for the pastor. | True False

10. The church planter must be strong willed person who is able to resist change as the new church grows. | True False

11. Strong personalities are needed at the inception of a business. | True False

12. Low structured management is most effective in established churches and businesses. | True False

13. High-structured management results in improved espirit de corps among employees of a business. | True False

14. Those who would start a new church must be motivated by successful pastors. | True False

15. Churches cannot be started apart from a divine miracle. | True False

16. God uses men of limited ability to overcome insurmountable problems in planting a new church. | True False

17. The church planter must be well known and influencial to be successful. | True False

18. The church planter will read the biographies of great men if he wants to be influencial. | True False

19. The church planter must balance tenacity and compassion in his ministry. | True False

20. The successful church planter will let his members provide leadership in the areas in which he is ignorant. | True False

21. The new church often reflects the weaknesses and strengths of the pioneer church planter. | True False

SECTION III

84 STEPS TO PLANT A CHURCH

The principles in this section present the ideal approach to starting a new church. These steps are a suggested strategy for church planting. But the author recognizes there are no perfect conditions for church planting, therefore there is no situation where these steps can be perfectly followed. These steps are similar to a road map, the driver like the chruch planter must apply his skills to the different conditions he faces at each point on his journey to safely arrive at his destination.

Although the 84 steps are designed for the pioneer church planter, they can be employed by the other five schools of church planting. As this manuscript was going to the printers, it was read by a group of laymen who were attempting to start a new church. Not only did it reveal some mistakes they had made, but the enormous task they faced. But most of all, they realized the necessity of a church planter.

Finally, everyone should realize there is no automatic success in planting a new church. A new endeavor can fail even when these steps are conscientiously applied. These steps are only practical helps to the man of God who is controlled by the Spirit of God in planting the church because he has been called by God.

CHAPTER 13

84 STEPS TO PLANT A CHURCH

Most church planters do not realize how much is involved in starting a church until they have done it. Often the church begins with no name, no building, no organ, or no stationary, and in most occasions, no prospects. "I didn't realize how much detail there was to getting a church started" commented Carl Godwin after founding the Bible Baptist Church of Lincoln, Nebraska. George Zarris founded the Fox River Valley Baptist Church in the Chicago area. Today he advises a young man to get the preparation work done before arriving on the field.

Is there a formula for starting a church? No! Just as there is no perfect man to start a church. Some men look for the perfect plan thinking they cannot fail if they have the successful blueprint. To ask for a pattern for church planting is like asking for a pattern for wrestling an alligator. The "criter" is so slippery and dangerous that the best advice is, "Don't get killed." But, there are some general principles however that church planters have used with success. The following suggestions are just that - suggestions. A church-planter may use all or none of them. They are not offered as a perfect sequence, but there is some logic to their order. They are offered to help the pioneer who has a lot of zeal but no sound strategy to get started. They may need to be adapted in different areas, but they represent ideas used by other successful church planters.

1. <u>The church planter must see the church in his mind.</u> Dr. Curtis Hutson, editor, <u>The Sword of the Lord</u>, has often said, "You can't achieve what you can't conceive." By that he meant, the man of God must have vision - he must have a vision of his work before he begins. The church planter must have a clear idea of his church before he arrives in the city to which God has called him. The planting and growth of Central Baptist Church (Milwaukee, Wisconsin) reflects the growth of its founder. The embryonic desires that built the church were planted and grew within James Martin in south Florida. I said in <u>The Ten Largest Sunday Schools</u> (Baker Book House, 1969), "The church was large in the heart of the pastor long before it was large on the street corner."

The creation of a church in the mind of the pastor is beyond natural explanation. That vision is divinely given. Jim Singleton left a growing church in Ohio to start Tri-City Baptist Temple in Tempe, Arizona. He later testified, "Until you have had God lead you, you can't explain the feeling of following him, yet the Lord led me to Arizona through that phone call from Louis Johnson."

Jeff Winstead fasted and prayed every Wednesday for a year before he went and planted Harvest Baptist Church in Hagerstown, Maryland. He prayed for many things and as he continued in prayer, the vision of the church became clear. Also, the place became clear. He prayed for a great chartering service and the offering for the building fund. When the offering was taken, over $8,000 came in, a miraculous gift considering the church was only ten weeks old.

2. <u>Be sure of your call from God</u>. The foundation of a New Testament church requires a man called by God, called to a city, and called to plant a church. If a man is going to start a church, he must be confident that God has led him to do so. The heartaches, pressures and hard work that is required in starting a church is so demanding that if the pastor does not have the inner assurance that God is the source of the church, then he will probably give up. James Martin testified, "I had always wanted to pastor a church. When I went to Jack Hyles' Pastors' School in 1969 the burden became so unbearable I could do nothing but look for a place to start a church." Rudy Holland remembers many times quitting would have been easy. "The assurance that God was going to do something in the Roanoke Valley through the Berean Baptist Church compelled me to keep pressing forward."

THE CALL OF GOD

1. A Burden (Mal. 1:1; Hab. 1:1)
2. A Desire (Jer. 20:9)
3. An Evidence of fruit (Jn. 15:16)

The <u>burden</u> for church planting is an internal pressure that comes to the church planter. Sometimes God uses natural means to lay a burden on a person's heart, such as a visit to a town or a man was stationed in the town when he was in military service. Sometimes the burden comes from reading about the need (no gospel church) in the town. One man went back to the town when he lived in sin, because no one told him of Christ. Other men have a burden for their home town because they know the spiritual need of an area. At other times the burden is supernatural. God just places a burden for a town and the man cannot shake it.

The <u>desire</u> for church planting is also an internal pressure that gets a man excited for an area, everytime he thinks about a town. When God has called a man to a town, he gets so excited about church planting that he thinks about it often and will not be satisfied until he gets there to start a church.

An <u>evidence of fruit</u> is the third part of the call of God. Unless a church planter has been used of God to win souls to church on a "one to one" basis, or been used to preach and see lost people walk an aisle, he is not ready to plant a church. An average minister cannot plant a church. The church planter must have the annointing of God to overcome the obstacles he will face.

Pastor Younge Chou, Full Gospel Church, Seoul, Korea (world's largest church) told me that a young man should not attempt to start a church until he had fasted and prayed for ten days. Chou explained that during these ten days the church planter would not only get God's annointing but would clearly see God's leading for the church.

Just as Barnabas and Paul were called of the Holy Spirit (Acts 13:2) to go and plant churches in Cyprus and Asia Minor, so the same Holy Spirit calls men to plant churches today.

3. <u>Be sure your wife is convinced</u>. George Zarris tells a young man that the most important ingredients in building a church are faith, works, and a helpmeet - "in that order." Grant Rice advises men not to start a church if their wife is not committed to the ministry. The pressures will be so great and quitting so easy. The author jokingly advises his students at Liberty Baptist Seminary, "Be sure you marry above yourself." By that he means that the wife will have some spiritual assets that the husband lacks, and when his give out, she can keep him going. But on the other hand, the church planter must have spiritual assets that are possessed by great leaders, for his greatest task is to lead.

4. <u>Be ready to preach and teach the Bible</u>. In days of compromise, people are looking for churches that preach the old-time gospel. The preaching of the Word of God is still the greatest enticement to get people into the house of God. Rudy Holland states, "I am convinced that every growing church must have a positive message. The Word of God gives a positive message, not only to the sinner but to the saint as well." The men who build great churches believe a message from God is the only hope for a lost, dying, hell-bound humanity. Therefore, they uphold the Bible as the authority for preaching and teaching. God's Word is the foundation of their churches.

Several church planters advise a young man to have

Notes

about six months of sermons prepared before they begin a church. Of course, a sermon must be "anointed by God" so the church planter can not just preach out of a notebook. If he can have the study completed and the outline prepared, the new church will get the best the church planter has to offer when he has the least amount of time to prepare.

Rev. Carl Bough, founder Calvary Heights Baptist Church, St. Louis, Missouri said "I had to preach for survival." He had planned to saved his best sermons for a time when the church was larger, but he had to preach his best to the small crowds in the beginning so he would have an opportunity to preach to larger crowds at a later time.

5. <u>Know your Ecclesiology</u>. No doctrine is more crucial to church planting than the doctrine of the church. The church is an assembly of baptized believers in whom Christ dwells under the discipline of the Word of God organized for evangelism, education, worship and fellowship, the administering of the ordinances and is reflected in spiritual gifts. When the author organizes a new church he explains that the church fits into the New Testament pattern as it (1) accepts only members who professed faith in Jesus Christ and have been baptized; (2) hold up the presence of the living Christ in their congregation; (3) place themselves under the discipline of the Scriptures; (4) be organized for evangelism, education, worship, fellowship; (5) administer the ordinances; and (6) exercise spiritual gifts of leadership needed to build a church.

Perhaps more new churches have failed at this point than any other place. Just as theology is the queen of all sciences, ecclesiology is the apex of theology. If there is any unbiblical deviation in theology, it becomes apparent in the doctrine of the church. Few argue over the doctrine of God or the nature of demons, but churches split over the authority or lack of authority by deacons, or storehouse tithing, or open communion verses closed communion.

God has a pattern for New Testament church polity, the closer one gets to the Biblical pattern of the church, the more likely he is to succeed in church planting.

Areas of Concern	Are You Clear?		
	Yes	No	?
1. Pastoral leadership			
2. Soul winning the ultimate priority of the church			
3. Baptism the door to church membership			
4. The Lord's Table only for baptized believers			
5. Storehouse tithing			
6. Deacons a serving office			
7. The autonomy of the local church			
8. The obligation of the church to world missions			
9. The Bible as the sole rule for faith and practice			
10. The congregation as the final authority in all matters			

Notes

6. Have a Biblical Philosophy of Ministry. Perry Purtle, founder of Canyon Creek Baptist Church, Richardson, Texas mapped out a clear strategy as to how he felt God wanted him to build the church. He began by setting long and short range goals. His formula for success can be summarized in four words: Plan--Organize--Execute--Control. Bill Monroe built a church in Florence, South Carolina by closely following the principles in Church Aflame. A right philosophy will keep you from getting sidetracked. Many young men from the Liberty schools have followed the philosophy of Thomas Road Baptist Church and when they have faced difficult decisions, they have had a context from which to decide. The same can be said of students from Hyles Anderson College, or Tennessee Temple schools. These graduates applied the strategy of Dr. Jack Hyles or Dr. Lee Roberson. The author was talking to Russ Merrin, who planted Heritage Baptist Church on Long Island about a problem. The author suggested "What would Jerry Falwell do?" The answer to the problem was immediately clear. Not that Jerry Falwell knew all the answers or did everything right, but the author helped Russ Merrin relate his problem to the total strategy he had been taught at Liberty.

7. Find the right city. Finding the right city, and in many cases, the section of a metropolitan city, is imperative. There are many steps by which God leads a young man to the place where he should start a church. Sometimes the call of God to plant a church comes before God leads him to a specific location. On other occasions, both the call and the location come at the same time. (a) A young man shall "set his face as a flint," which means he determines that he will plant a church if God has put it

Notes

upon his heart. Without this determination, he will flounder, or end up in some other form of Christian service. (b) Therefore, the church planter must resign all other options, such as taking a church or seeking employment while circumstances settle themselves. (c) Pray for the guidance of the Holy Spirit. Get a list of several needy cities and pray over them. (d) Wait for the Macedonian call. It will not be in a dream or vision for God does not reveal His will by these means today. But God speaks in the dark hours of the night as we wait upon Him in prayer. He gives an inner confidence that the world can never give. Sometimes the Macedonian call will come by a phone call or a letter inviting him to come start a church in an area. Sometimes it will be through circumstances or some form of an open door (I Cor. 16:9). The servant of the Lord must wait like Eliezer of Abraham who testified "I being in the way, the Lord led me" (Gen. 24:27). (e) Recognize that the calling of God to full time service is similar to the methods God uses to call a man to a city. A man knows he is being led of the Spirit when he has: (1) a spiritual burden for the city, (2) a lack of alternative locations. Jerry Falwell told a young man, "If you can go anywhere else, God is not leading you to Richmond." (f) Talk to men of God and ask them about the area and if they have any thoughts about your ability and the area where you are burdened. (g) Do not get to a place that is evangelized i.e., a large soul winning church or many New Testament churches. Go where there is a great need of the gospel. If a church planter is always competing with other gospel ministers he may lose his burden for an area, but a great need will keep him sharp in the work of the gospel.

Perry Purtle followed the principle of need: "I began looking for a place that was not populated with strong, fundamental churches. Need seems to be the greatest force in guiding a man to a city, however, need alone is not enough to draw a man to a city. Every area is needy no matter how many churches are in the town. There is no town in America that is over-saturated with the gospel. Every area has a multitude of unsaved, unchurched individuals. However, if there are New Testament churches in the area, there is a greater likelihood that the lost have at least have heard the gospel. Therefore, a young man is counseled to go start a church in one of the unchurched areas. (h) Pick a place that has great potential. Jewish neighborhoods need the gospel as well as the section where the super-rich live. But go to an area where you can lay a firm foundation, build a great church that will reach some in all sections of the area, including the Jews and the super-rich. (i) Go visit the area as soon as possible, especially before you move your family there. Get a map and become familiar with the area. Try to locate some prospects who are interested in planting churches in that area. (j) Take a community survey to get basic data on the area (see appendix).

8. <u>Determine to go first class.</u> When churches begin, there is rarely enough money to do everything perfect, but the pastor should determine to do everything as best as can be done. The location, advertising, music, preaching, etc. ought to be the best that can be offered. The pastor should dress correctly. The facilities should be bright and clean. In everything the church planter must strive for quality.

Jerry Bunch began Liberty Baptist Church in Orange County, California by renting a conference room in a plush hotel. Instantaneously the church had an image of excellence. If it had started in a store front, it would have had an image of mediocrity. Bunch realized the important principle of "first seed reference" i.e., a church will grow as it is planted. If you begin with a "store front" mentality, you will attract people who do not expect much. But if you begin with a high standard, you will attract quality personnel. It is true that lower class will attend a quality church, but the reverse is not true. A quality individual will not attend a "second rate" church.

Some fundamentalists believe sophistication and revivalism cannot be mixed. At the first anniversary of Canyon Creek Baptist Church, a symphony orchestra dressed in tuxedos provided the music. Sophistication was everywhere apparent. But when the congregation joined in singing "Oh, How I Love Jesus," a revival spirit filled the tent. When sinners walk an old fashion saw dust trail, the mixture of "first class music" and "spirituality" were evident.

9. <u>Have a positive attitude.</u> George Zarris felt lonely the first few weeks he started but testified, "As I told everyone I was starting a church, I suddenly realized I was somebody -- I was a child of the King. I was doing something no one else was doing. I was starting a church." That self-image supported him in his loneliness. Bill Monroe posted signs of a success motivational nature around his office area. Jerry Falwell constantly reminds students of Liberty Baptist schools, "Be power conscious, not problem conscious."

The pastor who constantly thinks he might fail, will probably fail. Yet, if God has called him, and if the Holy Spirit has led him, and if he has no unconfessed sin in his life, and if he has properly studied and prayed; he will succeed (Phil. 4:13).

10. <u>Start a pastor-led church.</u> The secret that will make your church different and successful from other fundamental churches in your area is leadership. "Everything rises or falls on leadership." Committee run churches (those controlled by the deacons) rarely

Notes

experience the growth of pastor-led churches. As a matter of fact, a committee, or a board of deacons have rarely planted a church. Because starting a church is such a gigantic step of faith, it is usually taken alone, not in concert with others. Therefore, men start churches, not committees.

When Joe Birdwell established the Twin Cities Baptist Church (St. Paul, Minnesota), he agreed to the establishment of an "advisory board" which made all the church decisions. Later, that board became a major source of problems resulting in a church split. Since the board has been disolved, Birdwell has been able to lead the church to grow. When Jim Singleton started Tri-City Baptist Church (Tempe, Arizona), he visited the homes of prospective members from other churches explaining that they did not have a traditional deacon controlled church. Those who did not like this did not join the church, sparing the church future problems.

11. <u>Do not neglect your walk with God</u>. The ministry is one of the easiest places to backslide. It is possible to become so involved in the ministry you can forget the basis of the ministry. Al Henson prayed daily for Nashville three years before he started Lighthouse Baptist Church. Jeff Winstead and his wife Audrey fasted and prayed one day per week for a year before starting Harvest Baptist Church (Hagerstown, Maryland). Jack Hyles preaches a sermon exhorting preachers to pray daily for wisdom, power and love. As a result, many have been motivated to include these three items on their daily prayer list.

12. <u>Be a soul winner</u>. A church must be built through soul winning. When a church planter starts from scratch, he must win all of his church members first. It is possible to plant a new church from a split off of another or by adding disgruntled members from surrounding churches. But, if the new church is not winning souls to church, it will eventually experience problems. The secret to growth in all areas is soul winning. The secret of building a church to 1,000 is to use the same principle General Motors uses to make a million cars. They build them one at a time. So a great church will be built as you win souls one at a time.

13. <u>Have Biblical standards for workers</u>. The temptation is starting a church is to use anyone until someone better comes along. But this is building your foundation on the sand, rather than a rock. Have biblical standards for workers in the church. Some young church planters think they can use anyone in a new church with a view of "preaching hard" in the future and raising the standards. The "first seed reference" of the church is predictive of its continuing ministry. It is almost impossible to overcome weaknesses built into a new church. The author includes an example of "standards for church workers" in <u>The Successful Sunday School and Teachers Guide Book</u> (Creation

House, 1980). Also, Jack Hyles has published the standards of First Baptist Church, Hammond, Indiana in <u>Let's Use Forms and Letters</u> (Sword of the Lord Publishers, 1966).

One church planter noted, "I taught all the teenagers and adults in one Sunday School class while my wife taught all the children in the other Sunday School class." He went on to explain he would rather have fewer classes and biblical workers, than add Sunday School classes that had to be taught by carnal workers. Not only should a church planter do this, but he should also tell his people why. This way the congregation is challenged to, (1) pray for workers, (2) qualify themselves or workers, and (3) have confidence in the pastor because he knows what he is doing. This way the congregation will not think the pastor is trying to keep all the jobs to himself.

14. <u>Learn from great men</u>. Greatness in the ministry is developed by associating and learning from other great men. The author has often called this the "hot poker" philosophy. The poker gets hot as its placed in the burning coals. James Mastin indicated three men taught him to be a leader. Jack Hyles taught him to preach hard, Verle Ackerman taught him the necessity of details and organization, and Al Janney gave him a pioneering spirit.

Someone has said the difference between what you are today and what you will be five years from now is the people you meet and the books you read. Carl Godwin graduated from a Nazarene college but today pastors an independent Baptist church after studying the ministries of Jack Hyles and Jerry Falwell. He testified, "Hyles taught me how to build a church, but Jerry challenged me to do it." George Zarris invited Grant Rice over to his apartment for a meal. Rice instructed Zarris on how to prepare a church constitution, how to choose an area and how to go about founding a church. Jim Singleton left the Southern Baptist Convention after fellowshiping with men like John R. Rice and pastors in the Ohio Baptist Bible Fellowship. Bill Monroe relied on the advice of Greg Dixon and Cecil Hodges. The successful church-planter is one willing to continue learning from great men.

Many successful church planters have told another man just starting to "phone me collect." The new church planter needs constant encouragement and when he faces trouble, he needs someone to whom he can go for counsel.

15. <u>Learn the biblical use of money</u>. The use of money in starting a church is more important than anything else except the use of people. In the final analysis, a leader's attitude toward people will influence the way he

handles finances. The Florence Baptist Temple has experienced phenomenal growth for many reasons. One of the church's strengths is Pastor Bill Monroe's attitude toward money. He sees there are two basic philosophies in church financing. First, management by *assets*. Many church leaders feel that as long as assets are greater than liabilities, a church can expand through deficit financing. These leaders have gone into excessive bond programs, purchasing more assets (building, property, buses, television equipment), always keeping their total debt under their total worth. As a result, their church has a good financial record on paper, but there is one problem. Many of these churches do not have weekly income to pay off their indebtedness. Some have gotten into bond trouble, having to sell off assets or face the embarrassment of not being able to pay bonds.

The second philosophy is *financing by cash flow*. This approach simply controls the spending so that a church will not obligate itself for more bonds or loans than its weekly offerings can presently liquidate, while at the same time, pay all of its operating expenses. This simple philosophy dictates that a church must have more cash income than outgo.

Monroe has built his church on cash flow. This has resulted in large facilities, respect from the financial community, confidence of the congregation and a sound basis on which to plan future growth. When asked for the secret to financing, Monroe gave the following guidelines he has followed in developing the financial program of the church.

16. <u>Don't badger the people for extra money</u>. Monroe believes in a New Testament principle of tithing and tries to get everyone to tithe. As a result, he does not take many extra offerings. Last year, he took one at Christmas for missions and another when they moved into the new building. Material possessions are always secondary in the Lord's work, but some churches have made it primary. He makes a man's relationship to Jesus Christ the most important ministry of his church. Then, if a man loves God, he will give out of obedience and love.

17. <u>Keep finances open</u>. Monroe makes a quarterly financial report to the congregation where all expenses are listed and explained to the congregation. However, staff salaries are not listed individually. Monroe indicates, "I don't think it is right to reveal a staff salary anymore than the other members in the church should reveal what they make." When people have a question about the finances, it is honestly approached and answered.

18. <u>Get an audited statement the first year</u>. The

business community has great respect for Florence Baptist Temple because Dal Felkel and Associates, a Certified Public Accounting firm, issues an annual audited statement which means an examination is made to determine the church's integrity and propriety in handling finances. As a result, the people give with confidence because they know an outside authority places its "stamp of approval" upon finances.

Many people do not trust a new church, and because of the mismanagement of independent Baptist churches, they may not have full confidence in <u>you</u>. Therefore, get an audited statement at the end of the first year. To get this accomplished, a CPA will have to be contracted during the first year of operations. When the statement is received, take it to the banker and other businesses with which you associate. It will get them confidence in the new church and will give credibility when going for a loan.

Monroe indicates a young preacher should get good financial advice from the business community. He indicates he does not always listen to his accountant, but to go against his accountant is a financial risk. His accountant has been right many more times than the financial advice he has received from fellow pastors or other interested friends in the church.

19. <u>Have a stewardship campaign the first year.</u> Bill Monroe indicates he learned from Jerry Falwell how to get yearly commitments from his people. A local restaurant is rented, and the people are charged a small cost for a meal. A good program is planned and a well known speaker is invited to bring the stewardship message. Prior to the banquet, the month of January is dedicated to emphasizing stewardship. Every Sunday School lesson as well as every sermon emphasizes giving money to God. Testimonies are given by laymen of how God has blessed them because they have tithed.

At the stewardship banquet, an audited report is given to every member along with a budget for the coming year. The people are presented with what they can do through tithing. "Their tithing has resulted in these buildings, equipment, property and they know that souls walk the aisle each week because they have given sacrificially. I don't have to beg them to give."*

20. <u>Expect a congregation to tihe from the first Sunday and a new Christian to tithe when he is first saved.</u> Many young church planters are reluctant to press their

---

*For more information on a stewardship campaign, see Truman Dollar, <u>How To Carry Out God's Financial Program</u> (Nashville, Tennessee: Thomas Nelson Publishers Inc., 1974).

Notes

people to tithe. thinking, it will run off potential members. Tithing is Christian (Malachi 3:10), therefore, expect all Christians to tithe. If a church is started with its members being aware of their financial obligation to God, the church will always have money problems. Carl Godwin had two years of problems in Lincoln, Nebraska, but the turning point was the stewardship campaign in the third year. He told the author he was considering leaving if something did not turn around. The stewardship campaign obligated the people to the church. Their financial obligation seemed to bring a renewed dedication in every area of life. New members joined and shortly thereafter, they purchased five acres of land and built. Now Godwin testifies that he ask every new member (whether a new Christian or by transfer of letter) to fill out a stewardship card. "If they are with the church in money, I know they are with the church in every area of ministry." Then Godwin confesses, "When we had problems, I wasn't able to ask people to give their all. I said it in preaching but denied it when taking the offering." To Carl Godwin, his changed attitude toward tithing is the key to the growth and stability of his church.

Some Baptist preachers make tithing only an obligation. But money is time and life. A man sacrifices his strength or time, getting a paycheck in return. This money is a man's life. Bill Monroe teaches his people that they are giving their strength or life back to God when they drop money in the offering plate. Their time and life is wrapped up in that envelope. Therefore, giving is the highest form of worship and we are giving ourselves back to God.

21. <u>Keep excellent financial records</u>. When the church first began, Monroe installed a bookkeeping system from Litton Business Systems throughout the church. Whereas, he could have purchased a small ledger book from a local secretary supply house for less than $5.00, he paid $400 for a complete system of books so the church would have accurate records. A full-time bookkeeper was employed when the church was running 400. Monroe advises a young pastor, "As soon as you can afford a bookkeeper, hire him." Monroe gets a financial report every Monday morning. He is never in the dark about the financial condition of the church.

22. <u>Cash on hand to operate four weeks</u>. As the author has studied many of the large churches, those most respected have cash on hand to operate on a business-like basis. Most of the churches that operate on cash flow have finances spread across several accounts so that if the money does not come in, the church's ministry is not threatened nor will they lose their testimony being unable to pay their bills. This is quite the opposite to some churches who have so extended themselves financially that the preacher has to run to the back of the auditorium to see if the offering is large

enough to cover the checks issued last Friday. Obviously, a new church cannot have four weeks of cash on hand as a reserve. But even a new church, can keep some on hand for last minute emergencies.

23. <u>Survey the town</u>. When Dr. David Stauffer received his Ph.D. from seminary in 1973, he wanted to start a church. He chose St. Louis because it was one of the top ten metropolitan areas in the nation, and, according to him, "The only town where there has never been a great growing fundamental church." He arrived in town, pulling all his furniture on a rental trailer. He stayed in a motel a week trying to find a place to start the Calvary Christian Temple. He did an urbanology chart projecting future density, traffic patterns, population growth, trying to find a neighborhood that would span from upper-class to lower-class people. He ultimately bought seven and one-half acres in the center of four expressways in South St. Louis County.

The church-planter should obtain the best city map available and mark all churches on the map, not forgetting those which are operating in homes, rented buildings, or have projected building plans. Rev. Everett L. Perry of the United Presbyterian Church suggests that churches of the same denomination should never be located closer than one and three-fourths miles from each other.

George Zarris drove to the Chicago area with Grant Rice looking for an area to start a church. He was looking for (1) a high population area; (2) an area that didn't have a growing fundamental church; (3) an area where land was available for future expansion, and (4) a place where they could rent a building or auditorium. Steve Frankenberger flew Zarris over the city of Aurora in his plane. They could not tell much from the air but, in that small plane with his wife, Barbara, George determined that Aurora was the area. Rice was not in the plane but had previously related the fact, "Fox River Valley will be the center of the population of the state of Illinois by 1980." The Sunday *Chicago Tribune* supported the decision with an article on the front page discussing a multi-million dollar shopping center in Aurora.

In larger cities statistical information can be gathered from a U.S. Census Report, the city librarian, the city engineer's office, or the local building inspector. The number of births in the area can be found by checking with the Public Health Department. The U.S. Census will reveal the age-group distribution. The principals of schools can give the percentage of children who are Protestant, Jewish or Catholic. If the area is not completely built up, local builders can help estimate how many houses will be eventually built in the area and what demand will be made for new houses. This information can also be obtained from city planners, building permit office, and realtors.

Notes

After you have determined the number of houses or dwelling units in the area, determine the average number of people in the area using the formula of 3.6 persons in each dwelling unit.

Some denominations maintain that a religious survey should be taken to determine church membership before a new church is considered for an area. However, church membership has no bearing on a man's relationship to God. Since liberal churches do not preach salvation, church-planters go to a city under the leadership of the Holy Spirit and begin knocking on doors, winning people to Jesus Christ.

Shippey believes that 2,000 to 3,000 persons of gross population per church is a safe rate for beginning the church. Carl Henry, Secretary of Survey and Research of the Board of American Missions, United Lutheran Church, states that he likes to consider 1,500 individuals to support a Protestant church in a metropolitan area.

Shippey feels a new church should not be started with less than 100 families. Many other denominations maintain that same ratio. However, fundamentalists have started with only one family. Some men have begun holding services with only their wives present. The eye of faith is sometimes greater than the mind of reason. Men have gone into a community to start a church under the leadership of God, knowing He would bless and people would come to the new endeavor.

The Jews in biblical times began a synagogue when 12 heads of families could reach an agreement to start a new congregation. This is a more realistic consideration for evangelistic churches today.

Not every neighborhood is conducive to starting a church. It is more difficult to start a church in an old established neighborhood than in a new suburban development. Whereas settled residents tend to have their membership in an old church, mobile families in new neighborhoods are prospects for church membership. Therefore, a growing neighborhood or a transient neighborhood provides a better opportunity for succeeding than an old neighborhood. Those who are mobile are eager to: (1) find new friends, (2) establish new patterns of life, and (3) adapt to a neighborhood. Mobile families suffer some culture shock. (Because of a disorientation to life around them, they search for stability. A church meets their existential need.) When a person goes through geographical mobility, he also undergoes psychological mobility; hence, he is a candidate for the gospel. Having been cut off from the stability of the past, he has greater needs. He could be won to Jesus Christ.

Some might criticize the principle of building a church in a neighborhood that is most conducive to the gospel. Yet,

Jesus commanded his disciples to go into a new city and if they were not received, shake the dust off their sandals (Matt. 10:14). Hence, Jesus was advocating that his disciples should endeavor to win those who are most receptive to the gospel and not invest as much time on those who would not receive the gospel. (He did not advocate avoiding those who were not receptive.) If a church-planter was seeking a location, he might spend more energies in a Protestant suburb rather than a Jewish neighborhood, knowing that he could win more to the Lord in one than the other. This does not mean he should never present the gospel to the Jews. The Bible teaches that Christ died for all and that "all have sinned and come short of the glory of God" (John 3:16; Rom. 3:23). Therefore, he should attempt to win all. But the greatest investment of his energies should be given those receptive to the gospel.

Many times those beginning independent churches become "star-struck" wanting to minister to the upper class or elite. However, money is often an insulation against the needs of life. It is hard for a rich man to enter the kingdom (Matt. 19:23,24); *hard* to get them saved, not impossible. At the same time, the poor are faced daily with the ultimate necessities of life; hence, they have a greater dependence on God's work in their life. Many times the poor will turn to Christ where the rich have a social snobbery and intellectual independence. A new church should minister among those most responsible to the gospel. Yet, it should not exclude the rich, nor aim only at the poor.

24. <u>Choose a name for the church</u>. The name of the church will outlast the pastor in most cases so its choice is of utmost importance. Grant Rice urges church planters to "say what you want to do" with your name. By this he means the name should identify with the field. When church planter Doug Porter named his church Valley City Baptist Church (Dundas, Ontario), he indicated a desire to reach beyond the town of Dundas into the other communities of the greater Hamilton Valley. Jerry Falwell advises pastoral students at Liberty Baptist schools not to follow his example in naming a church after a street address. Thomas Road Baptist Church has outgrown its Thomas Road address but the name will probably not be changed when the church moves to Liberty Mountain.

The name should also identify the nature of the church. When the author organizes a new church, he always urges them to call themselves "Baptist." His reasons for this are explained above in the section on "The Theology of Naming a Church."

Notes

```
Choosing a Church Name

1.  Spiritual Identity
2.  Geographical Identity
3.  Reflective of the Church's Aim
```

     a. Central Baptist Church, Milwaukee because it was central to the city.

     b. Tri-Cities Baptist Church, Gladstone, Oregon, because it had a ministry to the three major cities in South Portland.

     c. New Life Baptist Church, Harrisburg, PA because the church offered new life in Christ.

     d. Shenandoah Valley Baptist Church, Winchester, VA Although not located immediately in Winchester, it has a ministry to all in the north valley.

     e. Calvary Heights Baptist Temple, St. Louis because the church is on a hill and because Calvary is the foundation of Christianity.

     f. Liberty Baptist Church, Irvine, CA because the gospel frees a man and because the pastor wanted to identify with Dr. Jerry Falwell.

     g. Twin Cities Baptist Church because the church was located between St. Paul and Minneapolis and wanted to minister to both cities.

    25. <u>Get a local address.</u> As soon as you know where you will start the church, establish a local address. Most men will open a post office box and have people sending mail there. Some have used a post office box for six months before the church was actually begun. A local address is needed to incorporate, open a bank account, etc. and will identify the church in the neighborhood.

    26. <u>Have a promotional picture made.</u> For the cost involved it is probably better to consult a commercial photographer. The commercial photo will be treated with a high gloss finish which will reproduce better in your literature. Have a photograph made of both you and one with your family.

    27. <u>Get a nonprofit permit number.</u> While at the post office, obtain a nonprofit permit number. The post office will explain the regulation for use of the permit. Zip codes are essential for bulk mailing. Most post offices will not grant the nonprofit permit until you are incorporated however, regulations vary because some states do not incorporate churches.

28. <u>Find a place to live</u>. While some men have arrived in a rental truck and started the church the next Sunday, it is usually best to settle your family first. If they are happy, then they will support you in planting the church. The author laughs when he remembers a man who arrived in a rental truck and left his wife in the cab at the curb while he went door to door inviting people to his church. While we may admire his zeal, we surely think less of his common sense. By the way, his church failed.

The author has often said the church planter should buy a house. If he has never gone through the experience of purchasing a home for his family, it will be difficult for him to lead a spiritual family to purchase land and build. He will learn invaluable lessons in locating financing, mortgages, etc.

29. <u>Open a church bank account</u>. The day after he named the church, George Zarris opened a bank account at the first bank they saw in Aurora, Illinois, the place where the new church was to be founded. An account should be opened in the name of the church long before the first service of the church. Many times, the church-planter will have to sign the checks until a treasurer is elected at the organizational/charter service. However, at the chartering meeting, a vote will be taken to incorporate the checking account with its assets and liabilities into the new church. So even before the church begins, he is financially accountable to the church he will start.

30. <u>Receive money up to six months before the church begins</u>. As soon as a new church's city, name and approximate date of beginning is known, the church planter should begin receiving money into the checking account. There may be some people in the area who have been praying for the new church who will give to the project. The church planter will have parents, relatives, and friends who pray for him. They may want to make a financial gift to the new church and the new bank account provides a means. However, they should be advised to tithe to their present responsibility. Also, the church planter may want to send personal gifts ahead to begin the work. Some even begin to divert their tithe before arriving at the location. Once again the danger of now recognizing the priority of the tithe is a danger. For the church planter who wants the full blessing of God on his work and the full support of the church where he is presently serving, he should be faithful with his tithes there until God leads him to make a change.

Some of the greatest expenses for starting a new church come in the first months; moving, rent deposit on an apartment/rent, printing, advertisement, etc. Therefore, the church planter should prepare a realistic budget for the first months expectations and begin raising money to meet the need.

Notes

31. <u>Receipt all money</u>. The church planter will need to secure a receipt book that has the name of the church printed on the receipt, plus a sequence of numbers. Each gift must be recorded and a receipt issued. These records became a part of the new church's financial books. When the church is actually chartered, individual receipts will not be given on a weekly basis, but members will have their gifts posted in a receipting journal.

32. <u>Plan a three month's budget</u>. The church planter will have to approximate all the expenses he will incure in the first 90 days and make this a prayer goal. This becomes a realistic prayer challenge to share with churches and friends.

Preparing a budget for a nonexistent ministry is difficult but necessary. A budget is necessary to good financial management. Money is ministry. The way you handle the money is the way you handle the ministry. The following simple rules will help the young preacher starting out.

```
BASIC FINANCIAL RULES
1. Do not spend more money than you take in.
2. Income should increase in proportion to membership.
3. Always know how much money you have in all accounts.
4. Keep good credit in the community, pay all bills on time.
```

When preparing the first budget, there are certain things to remember. First include your moving expense. The cost of moving is great regardless of how you do it. Also, the cost of housing should be considered. In the long run, buying your own home is cheaper than renting. Grant Rice advises men to buy an older home as they have more space and that space may be needed for church meetings at the beginning. When considering your personal budget, remember to include everything. Pastors are entitled to certain tax breaks with regard to housing, car allowance and insurance. Keep these in mind as you prepare your personal budget.

Notes

```
┌─────────────────────────────────────────────────┐
│           Budget                    Estimate    │
│  1. Moving expenses                             │
│     (Trailer rental, travel, meals,             │
│     incidentals)                 $ _____     │
│  2. Deposit for rent, phone,                    │
│     utilities, etc.                _____     │
│  3. Home rent for 90 days.         _____     │
│  4. Church rent for 90 days.       _____     │
│  5. Printing for brochures.        _____     │
│  6. Postage                        _____     │
│  7. Advertisement                  _____     │
│  8. Salary                         _____     │
│  9. Utilities                      _____     │
│                                                 │
│              90 Day Total        $ _____     │
│           needed per month       $ _____     │
└─────────────────────────────────────────────────┘
```

After the church planter sees the expenses of starting a church, he may want to quit. Perhaps no other reason has killed new churches than lack of financial planning. If the church planter can realistically see the cost, and continue with plans, then maybe that is an indicator that God is calling him.

33. <u>Raise financial support</u>. Just as the foreign missionary must raise his support before going to the field, so must the church planter. The one exception is that the church planter will soon pastor a church that is self-supporting. Most church planters ask for financial support for six months to one year. Many are willing to take on a short term responsibility for church planting but resist a life-long obligation.

George Zarris sent out letters asking for money from friends. While it did not work well for Zarris, Dave Barton notes money received from this source was all the salary he had when starting his church in Herdon, Virginia. Today, he advises young men to have their pastor write a letter for financial support.

Also, many pastors are eager to help men start churches. Several fellowships exist primarily to raise funds for new churches including the Baptist Bible Fellowship (Springfield, Missouri), Lighthouse Fellowship (Nashville, Tennessee) and Liberty Baptist Fellowship for Church Planting (Roanoke, Virginia).

    a. Send prayer letters to relatives and friends of the church planter. A brochure of the new work should be enclosed.

Notes

      b. Solicit like faith churches for monthly support, or the opportunity to make a presentation so the church can give a one-time offering.

      c. Some church planters schedule their prayer meetings on another night than Wednesday so that during the first few months he can travel to other churches to raise support.

      d. If the church planter is leaving school, his friends may pledge financial support.

      e. The home church or sponsoring church may provide monthly support, or other support such as hymn books, printing, musical instruments, amplifications, office equipment, etc.

      f. A local fellowship of Baptist churches/pastors may offer to support the church planter.

    34. <u>Incorporate as soon as possible</u>. Except in West Virginia and Virginia where a church cannot be incorporated, this step should be done as soon as possible. Call legal aid and ask for a lawyer's help in organizing the church. Many older fundamental churches will have an attorney who might perform this fee gratis. Costs will vary from state to state and in some states a church can be incorporated without a lawyer. Carl Godwin waited a month after the first service to contact a lawyer. Some have incorporated before the first service. State incorporation makes the church a legal entity that can own property, physical assets and assume debt. This step should not be confused with chartering or the organizational service which is recognition of the spiritual entity of the new church.

    35. <u>Contact friends in the area</u>. When a man returns to his hometown, he has a number of prospects among his old friends, relatives, etc. Upon returning to Lincoln, Nebraska, Carl Godwin got out his high school annual *The Link* and put his old high school buddies on his mailing list. As he began visiting, a former friend, Doug Gregg and his wife, Carolyn, received the Lord. These people encouraged Godwin to go on with plans to begin the church.

    36. <u>Get an IRS number for taxable giving</u>. The church should be registered as a charity as soon as possible. Also, a Social Security disclaimer should be filed if the pastor does not intend to participate in this program. Contact these offices for the appropriate forms and instructions.

    37. <u>Begin gathering prospects</u>. Prospects include anyone who is not attending a church, but could and should attend your church. They can be found in several places. Some men have used the mailing lists of radio/television

ministries. James Mastin got his first prospect from a church on the other side of town from where he began his ministry. Danny Smith met a resident of Richmond while working on staff at Thomas Road Baptist Church in Lynchburg. Carl Godwin got seventy names from a union membership list where his father was a member. He also contacted old friends.

> Get names of prospects (find every available person).
> a. Address of friends and relatives
> b. Newcomers' list
> c. Former high school acquaintances (if pastor is returning to hometown)
> d. Names of unchurched friends given by people in other churches
> e. Community canvass
> f. Door to door visitation
> g. Ask for a phone response on mailings and other advertisements
> h. Get names of other potential members from those who attend "Get Acquainted Meeting"

38. <u>Prepare a church constitution</u>. A sample constitution is included in the appendix of this manual that can be used with minor adaptations to each local need. Most young churches will not have knowledgeable Christians who can prepare this document. Also, the church-planter will usually know more about the business affairs of the church than any other in the congregation. Therefore, he should prepare the constitution and bylaws before he arrives on location. The document should be printed and distributed to potential members. They should be given opportunity to discuss it at a prayer meeting or in the Adult Sunday School Class. The congregation will vote its approval at the chartering/organizational meeting. Since the church is a young group, the pastor should give leadership in getting this time-consuming job done.

39. <u>Choose a first location</u>. After finding the part of the city where to minister, the next task is finding a building for services. Most new churches must rent facilities. For this purpose, most pastors first look for public school facilities. Perry Purtle gives the following guidelines: "After determining in what area of the city I wanted to build, I then looked for a Sunday meeting place as near as possible to the area where I wanted to build. I went to the public school and rented the auditorium, where we met for a year." The second best place is a motel with a large assembly/convention room. These rooms are seldom busy on Sunday morning and the manager will usually rent the room on a continuing basis.

Notes

> **THINGS TO LOOK FOR IN TEMPORARY FACILITIES**
>
> Auditorium with enough available:
> 1. Seating
> 2. Rest rooms
> 3. Parking
> 4. Heating and cooling
> 5. Piano
> 6. Loud speaker system
> 7. Smaller rooms available for Sunday School rooms
> 8. Smaller room available for nursery
> 9. Telephone
> 10. Water fountain

Most of these qualities are found in public or private schools and motels. Others have used any facility available: YMCA, lodge hall, firehouse, restaurant, civic auditorium, house, carport, factory, recreation center, or funeral home. Get a definite commitment on the building as to when you can begin services and what the rent will be. Find out what storage space you can use at the building for hymnbooks, pulpit and supplies.

40. <u>Use the mails</u>. Every time you meet someone that is interested in the new church, put their name on your mailing list. First, send them a letter inviting them to the church with a brochure. Then begin sending a regular newsletter to them promoting the new church.
You will not be able to see everyone on a regular basis, but your newsletter can go into every home telling them what God is doing in the new church. Do not use the newsletter to preach to them. Share the excitement of the work and they may get excited.

> **THINGS TO PLACE IN THE NEWSLETTER**
>
> 1. Attendance (compare so growth can be seen)
> 2. Offerings (show accumulation offerings so strengths can be seen)
> 3. Conversions
> 4. New items purchased
> 5. New aspects of the ministry
> 6. Have special days and promote them
> 7. Share goals and dreams

41. <u>Get hymnbooks and offering plates</u>. These items are easy to forget until you need them in the first service. Some churches have older hymn books and offering plates they will give or loan to a new church. Dallas Billington, pastor of Akron Baptist Temple began many new churches and he always donated new hymn books to each church. Care should be taken to select a hymnbook that includes the hymns that are sung in fundamental churches. Some hymn books may be donated that include a predominate number of hymns used in liturgical

worship services. Then the presence of the hymn books, even though free, are not an asset to the new church.

42. <u>Saturate the community</u>. Use every available means to reach every available person at every available time. Announce the beginning of the church over television, radio, billboards, newspapers, buses, etc. Rev. Ken McCormack, Tri-City Baptist Temple, Gladstone, Oregon, effectively uses ads on bus benches at the bus stops throughout the area.

43. <u>Buy an offset printing press</u>. Perhaps the first purchase by the church should be a printing press. The Communists and cults have used the printing press to get their message out. During the 1960's the crude mimeograph machines of the underground press forced our nation out of Viet Nam. An A. B. Dick offset will be suitable for most printing needs. These can often be purchased in good used condition. Having your own press will cut costs and time delays in getting brochures and newsletters printed. Your new church should learn the power of the press.

44. <u>Purchase an automatic address machine</u>. The second purchase should be some type of addressing machine to quickly get out your mailings to the public.

45. <u>Set ministry goals</u>. Most successful church planters set short, medium and long range goals. Generally, these goals aid in setting direction and measuring progress. Some church planters set goals of how many members they would have at the end of the first year, because an attendance objective drove them to diligent work. Others knew they would work with every ounce of strength; they did not need goals.

```
                GOALS FOR A NEW CHURCH
   1. Visits made.              6. Fifty in the service.
   2. Prospects on mailing      7. Large chartering
      list.                        service offering.
   3. Number present on         8. Number baptized at
      soul winning                 first baptismal
      visitation.                  service.
   4. Number of conversions.    9. Offering to reach
                                   $10 per attender.
   5. Number of charter        10. Offerings to reach
      members.                     weekly budget.
```

46. <u>Set a goal to make it</u>. When can a church planter tell if his church will make it? Jerry Falwell

Notes

says "He knew in his heart before he began that he would make it because God had called him." Yet there are three stages in the growth of a church when the church planter will reach a plateau. When he makes each one, he will move on to new stability.

> 1. When the offerings cover all weekly expenses. (The church no longer lives on money from outside sources.)
> 2. When the church purchases a piece of property. (The church is no longer a gypsy in the community.)
> 3. When the church builds and moves into its first building. (The church is part of the community.)

The church-planter should set a goal to reach all three of these goals, for the church has not made it until he has done all three. When writing stories on the graduates of Liberty who had begun churches, Dr. Falwell told the author not to print them on former students who had not built a building because they had not yet made it. Even those who buy old church buildings or convert other types of buildings into church buildings are not fully accepted into the community as a church that builds.

47. <u>Design a logo</u>. Commercial institutions use a logo as a symbol to advertise their company. The golden arches possess special significance to hamburg lovers everywhere. A logo can and should be used by a church to accomplish similar results. Most church planters choose one they have seen on other churches that had meaning to them.

48. <u>Adopt a slogan</u>. People will identify a church by its reputation and a good slogan can help shape that reputation. Valley City Baptist Church was characterized as "The People-Loving Church" in its advertising in Dundas, Ontario. "The Valley's Most Exciting Church" appeared in most Berean Baptist Church literature as it was started in Roanoke, Virginia. The people of Lincoln, Nebraska were urged to "Discover the Difference at Bible Baptist Church."

49. <u>Get an outside temporary church sign</u>. Even if the only sign you can use is a portable sign, a well painted sign is a good advertising tool. If a permanent sign can be posted at your meeting place, that is of course better. Be sure to include the church's name, times of services and a phone number for further information. The Central Baptist Church of Milwaukee, Wisconsin used a large sandwich board in front of the YMCA they rented, so did the Bluewater Baptist Church, Sarnia, Ontario.

50. <u>Get an inside sign</u>. When guests come into your building, have a large poster/sign that identifies the church, pastor with logo and motto. A public school room or motel auditorium can be cold and indifferent. The church needs something to focus attention on the Lord Jesus Christ and the new church that is being formed.

51. <u>Print and distribute brochures and fliers</u>. Get brochures and fliers printed immediately. They should include information on the pastor, the doctrine of the church and the type of program the church will offer. Order early, for printing requires time. (Carl Godwin had 3,000 printed, handed out 2,000 and mailed 400.) A letter could be included with the flier. The old addage is still true, "You never get a second opportunity to make a first good impression." The brochure should be first rate because prospects will judge the new church by their first impression and that will be the brochure. They will not have a church building to tell them what type of church the new one will be, there has not been a church service by which they will make a judgment. So make the brochure colorful, exciting, yet informative.

FIRST BROCHURE
1. Name of church
2. Basic information (location, time, place)
3. Brief doctrinal statement
4. Pastor's name and picture
5. Pastor's accomplishments and education (To show church is not a "fly-by-night" idea)
6. Services of church (nursery, youth programs, etc.)
7. Plans (immediate and long range). People must be able to identify with pastor's vision.
8. Credibility (letter from sponsoring church, Jerry Falwell, or other well-known minister, or support by Baptist Bible Fellowship, Liberty Baptist Fellowship for Church Planting)

---

52. <u>Visit door to door</u>. When Jerry Falwell began Thomas Road Baptist Church, he first went door to door in a six block area surrounding the church. As that was canvassed, the area was expanded until eventually he had visited the entire town several times. Today he advises young pastors to do the same when starting their churches. Falwell did not spend a great deal of time in any one home. He made a friendly call; informing the people of the church, then inviting them to the service of the church. He

left literature and when he found interest in his church, he made a note and returned to call on them again.

53. <u>Get help visiting</u>. A youth group or Sunday School class from a sponsoring church can help visiting the area, distributing fliers and inviting people to the first service. Recently Rev. Ken Chapman of Liberty Bible Institute took several students with him to Gettysburg, Pennsylvania to organize a new church. The students visited on Saturday and helped out in the services on Sunday. One Bible college in Florida sent over 200 students to the St. Petersburg's area to canvess an area where a new church was forming.

54. <u>Hold get acquainted meetings</u>. George Zarris in Aurora, Illinois, held two or three Tuesday night meetings before he began his church. During the preceeding week he would visit forty to sixty hours inviting people to these meetings. At the meeting the young pastor presented his vision to the people in a very casual way. The gospel was presented but no pressure to "walk an aisle" was applied. Most pastors who use this approach can gather a nucleus of interested people. These people may be in a liberal church, a dead conservative church or completely unattached to a church. The main thing a church planter can do in these meetings is share his burden and vision. Some people in dead churches may want the exact type of church that he is presenting. Also by not conflicting with regular church meetings, the prospect is not forced to make a choice against his present church, yet.

55. <u>Begin prayer meeting on an off right</u>. Gather the new church for prayer and Bible study on a Tuesday or Thursday. This has two benefits. First, members of other churches who are looking for a fundamental church can visit without missing a service at their church. Also, this allows the pastor to visit other churches to raise money at the beginning.

56. <u>Place a newspaper ad for the first service</u>. The successful church planter will learn how to advertise in the newspaper. There should be a well laid out ad for the first service. Be sure to include all the pertinent information, church name, time, place, etc. Also, church ads do more than advertise the time and place of meetings. Paid-for space is used to share news, growth, philosophy, and new items in the church. Once the ad read: "When driving by--watch our new building go up." On another occasion: "Sorry we couldn't seat everyone last Sunday evening. Our new auditorium is on the way." Again, "Our new singles class is busting at the seams." During a session on the Christian home, the church planter can advertise his topic and philosophy of the Christian family.

57. <u>Secure offering envelopes and visitors cards.</u>
Many churches have these forms printed with the church name. This may be an unnecessary expense, but it shows the church planter's commitment. Offering envelopes are a necessity. These can be ordered from regular suppliers. One church planter testified, "When a new member takes a box of envelopes and begins to use them the following week, I knew they are with us." Too many church planters have been too reluctant to ask for money and have not obligated his people to the new church.

58. <u>Post fliers.</u> Most grocery stores, laundramats, and convience stores have a community bulletin board. They will allow you to post a flier in their window.

59. <u>Use cable TV.</u> Many communities are serviced with cable TV. These stations are interested in local programing. You can advertise your church free as a "community event." Also, some local talk show programs may be interested in interviewing you as a local leader.

60. <u>Send out public service announcements.</u> Hundreds of free advertising spots are given out daily by most radio stations to charitable and educational organizations. However, you must send announcements of the upcoming event at least one week in advance. Type the announcement as a press release. (See Appendix)

61. <u>Write press releases.</u> Write a press release for the local papers. Take it rather than mail it to the church editors. The small weekly community papers are more likely to print it than the large metropolitan dailies. For a sample press release, see the Appendix.

62. <u>Do not publically attack other pastors and churches</u>. As soon as you begin the church, there will be those who disagree with the new church. Liberal churches will oppose its theology and fundamental churches will disagree that a need exists and will judge the church planter's motives in starting a church. Shortly after Rudy Holland began, one local newspaper reported, "Members and ministers of other churches are jealous of the independent super-aggressiveness. They dismiss it as superficial at best; robbery at worst." Many in town called Bill Monroe a "Pentecostal Baptist" because of the enthusiastic singing, evangelistic preaching and rebaptizing of church members who are saved in the church. Some of the churches in the city publically criticized the Fox River Valley Baptist Church. Zarris rationalizes, "Every time they criticize us, they advertise our ministry. Their people come to see what we are all about." When a lady joined the church and requested her letter, the pastor attacked the Fox River Valley Baptist Church from his pulpit. Zarris thought to himself, "How foolish. Since he's not doing anything, he is telling dissatisfied Christians that we *are* doing something."

Notes

Notes

The purpose of the new church is not to correct the other churches, and he cannot do it even if he tried. Also, it is not one church's duty to attack another, for it seldom helps them and always hurts the attacking church. The church-planter/pastor should resist the temptation to fight fire with fire. He only has twenty-four hours in his day, and these should be used to win souls and build his church.

63. <u>Be proud of the people in a new church</u>. A pastor should never be apologetic about his people, no matter how few or how young they may be in the Lord. Bill Monroe considers his church and the people of that church as very special. "I feel possessive about my church because I have given it birth. It is hard to separate the church from my thinking and feeling. If someone criticizes my people, that's a criticism of me. When someone calls us arrogant, I am defensive." Monroe explained that he has tried to build pride into his people. "I was proud of this church when we had only 30. I was never ashamed of the old dilapidated theater building. Even in those early days when we had some marginal special music, I was proud of them because they were my people." The church continued to grow because of the deep respect that Monroe had for his congregation. "I never met a rich or dignified person that I couldn't honestly invite to our services."

64. <u>Talk about each success and forget about each failure</u>. A church planter will have to rejoice over small victories and count his growth in small steps. A church moves forward from victory to victory, not by reliving the agonies of each defeat. The young pastor should promote the successes in the church so as to encourage new converts. One church has posted a large sign consisting of three columns of statistics: (1) souls sought, (2) souls brought and, (3) souls saved. The first column indicated how many visits were made; second, how many attended Sunday School; and third, those who have accepted Christ as Saviour.

A new church should be victory conscious, not obstacle conscious. When God puts a vision in the heart of a church planter, it is for the "big view" therefore, he must know where he is going and encourage his people everytime they take a step toward that goal.

65. <u>Share vision with the people.</u> Everything worth while is built on dreams, whether its a marriage, a college education or a new church. People will work, give sacrificially, and put up with temporary facilities if they have a dream of where they are going. To move the people, the church planter must share his vision/dreams with his people.

One April morning while shaving, Jim Singleton had a burden on his heart. He told his wife, "The Lord wants us to start an academy...this fall." When he told the people, they agreed, but *this fall* stretched their faith. Yet, they voted by faith to proceed, because of their common dream to reach the area.

Rudy Holland has tried to instill an attitude of growth in his people. Anything other than expansion would be a traumatic experience to the infant congregation. So every time he challenges them to construct a new building, they have responded to his leadership.

66. <u>Plan well the church services</u>. Just because there is a small crowd is no reason to run the church meeting out of one's hip pocket. Plan each church service in an organized manner. Rudy Holland explains, "I do not mean formalism. Many independent Baptists pride themselves on being unorganized. This can be a real detriment to a new church. People will follow only if they are assured that the leader knows where he is going. A poorly organized church service usually indicates a poorly organized church."

If the ushers, pianist, and those taking part in special music have an order of service and they are confident, the news will soon spread to the congregation that the pastor is prepared to lead them.

67. <u>Have informal services</u>. The music may not be the best in a new church, so make sure the singing communicates the gospel to people's hearts. People are sick of highly formal worship services. Rudy Holland observes, "It is wise to be careful of the type music used. Remember, starting with "sangin" that is sung through the nose will make it difficult to improve the music later. I recommend that good solid music be chosen. In the early days of a church, there may be little music used. It is better to have no music at all in a new church than to have music which does not glorify Christ."

68. <u>Receive an offering the first Sunday</u>. Some pastors are reluctant to receive an offering particularly if the crowd is small and the new church is heavily underwritten. But what is done in that first service will establish a pattern. There are four principles to remember in receiving an offering.

    a. Point out the financial need. The church planter may mention the need for rent, advertisement, hymn books, or any number of things, but let the people know the financial need.

    b. Encourage every person to have a part in the offering. There are very few people who cannot give; therefore, ask everyone to have a part in the offering, even the children. A small child can have the satisfaction of helping build a new church. This will not only increase

Notes

the offering, but will make everyone feel he can participate in this part of the service. Never fear asking for money. Remember, people are being asked to avail themselves of the blessings of God (Mal. 3:10).

    c. Give every person an offering envelope. This encourages people to give because it provides a confidential means of giving. Many people would be embarrassed to let others see what they drop in the plate. Also, explain to people they should have a record of their giving so they can evaluate the extent of their giving. Are they giving what they should? Since God keeps records, so should your people. Then they have records for income tax.

    d. Remind the people that the money is given to God. Tell every person to ask God what he would have him give. As pastor, point out that God knows the financial need; he knows what part each of your people should have in the offering. If all are obedient to God, they will be blessed and the need will be met.

    69. <u>Start a Sunday School</u>. From the very beginning, the church planter must realize that Sunday School is the agency to build a church, "reaching...teaching...winning...training." The church planter will want to meet weekly with all the teachers, giving them instruction in both content and methodology. He will personally recruit all teachers, stressing qualifications: salvation, church membership, tithing, attendance, pupil visitation, and separation from the world.

    Start with three classes in Sunday School: (a) Adult (youth and older); (b) Primary; (c) Nursery (Carl Godwin made a big deal out of the nursery, even in his first flier. To do this, some furniture and cookies are needed); and (d) Add the Junior class later.

    70. <u>Follow up visitors</u>. Have a follow-up letter ready to send to all visitors who attent the first Sunday. Also, make an attempt to get into the houses of visitors within a few days. The church planter's wife can phone during the day, especially if a family visited the new church. A woman to woman contact will not only be personal but effective.

    71. <u>Print a church newspaper</u>. When Jerry Falwell started his church, he sent out a weekly church newspaper each week. While increased postal rates and growing stability make a weekly paper unnecessary later on, it is imperative in the first few months. Later, a monthly paper could be used effectively by the new church.

    72. <u>Teach church distinctives</u>. Church members will

come from a variety of different backgrounds. They will
need to understand the Baptist distinctives and the soul
winning aim of a New Testament church. Therefore, the church
planter must also be an educator to teach. Actually, the
pastor should use his Wednesday night prayer meetings and
Sunday evening services to teach the distinctives of the
new church. Many church planters have testified that these
series on church polity were among the best they ever
preached. Perhaps it was the need that every one felt
in the new church to do things correctly. Therefore, they
searched the Scriptures carefully to find what God had to
say about church polity. Some new churches establish a
local church Bible Institute on Sunday evenings before
the sermon to teach Bible doctrine and principles of the
Christian life to new converts. This trend appears to be
replacing the traditional SBC Training Union, particularly
in independent churches.

73. <u>Gather a qualified staff</u>. In a small church
the music, youth and Sunday School will be guided by
laymen since the church lacks finances for full-time
assistance. However, Perry Purtle reported, "I determined
to build a staff before I built a building. People will
come because of our well-rounded program, not because of
our building. The best money I can spend is on a staff
member. I will borrow money to hire a staff, if necessary.
I called a full-time co-worker the first week. When we were
one year old, I had five on the staff; three were full
time and two part time." Not everyone agrees with
Dr. Purtle, but no one can argue his success. He called
his long-time friend, J. E. Hughes, to help begin the
church and the two made a pact to share equally the
finances that came in.

74. <u>Begin a building fund</u>. The author always takes
an offering at the chartering/organizational service for a
new church. He has usually challenged the people to a goal
that stretched the faith of the new congregation. He has
reminded the people "This community will not accept you as a
reputable church until you have your own property and
building. In beginning this fund for a new building you
are gaining credibility."

Church	Goal	Amount
Bible Baptist Church, Sumpter, SC	$ 800	$ 800.00
Central Baptist Church, Victoria, VA	2000	2000.56
Twin City Baptist Church, St. Paul, MN	2000 +	2050.00
Harvest Baptist Church, Hagerstown, MD	3000	8000.11

Notes

Open a savings account at the bank for a building fund. This will show the people you intend to remain in town. Also, money raised can be used for down payments on land and/or build without the need for a special down payment offering. Jeff Winstead raised over $20,000 in his building fund in the first four months of the churches existance. This gave the young church credibility in the mind of local businessmen.

75. <u>Establish a visitation program</u>. The question is often asked, What type of visitation program builds a new church? Some maintain that soul-winning is the basis of building a church, and a young man should go out to lead people to Christ. Others feel that a new church needs exposure. Therefore, the church planter should enlist as many helpers to contact as many people as possible, inviting them to the new church.

The first is called soul winning evangelism and the second is called friendship evangelism. Some great soul-winning churches have been established by both methods, so neither excludes the other. By soul-winning visitation, new babes are brought into the church. This is the purpose of the church. But house-to-house visitation will find mature Christians who may be languishing in dead churches. Older Christians can give money, teach classes and win souls. Rudy Holland balances these programs and win souls. He Holland balances these contrasting opinions. "The visitation program will net those people who have been made aware of your church as a result of advertising. Your church should have an active visitation program, teaching soul-winning as a vital part of visitation. Emphasize every visit primarily as a soul-winning call and only secondarily as a church prospect call."

Should the church-planter spend his time winning new converts or recruiting older Christians? When Carl Godwin was interviewing pastors before beginning his church in Lincoln, he asked about the foundation of a new church. Some pastors told Godwin not to proselyte older Christians from other churches because they had poor church habits and were usually the malcontents. "Go door-to-door and win your whole congregation to Christ," one pastor told Godwin, "Then you have a church that will be pure and zealous to serve Christ." The older pastor continued, "These new Christians will follow your leadership and you can build a church without friction."

When Godwin founded Calvary Bible Church in Lincoln, he changed his thinking. His young Christians were not trained to come to Sunday services. They did not tithe, and some had problems with sins. These new babes in Christ were a thrill to Godwin, but they were not stable enough to help build a church. God sent the church some mature Christians from other churches who could lead souls to Christ and teach Sunday School. These were not malcontents, but were Christians who had been praying for an aggressive soul-winning church in their city.

On the other hand, while Godwin was interviewing another pastor, one directed him to get a nucleus of mature Christians to add stability to the young congregation. Some new churches are built almost exclusively on older Christians. These churches are founded by groups that have come out of another church, perhaps to preserve pure doctrine or to repudiate sin in the former assembly. These churches usually do not grow rapidly but do a commendable job of ministering the Word of God.

Sometimes, older Christians have the stability of time-proven endurance, but they lack the zeal of the young convert who is carried along by his love for Christ.

Some church planters who have spent all their time on soul-winning, complain they can lead people to Christ at the front door of a home but can not get them to attend church. The church planter from Baptist Bible College, Springfield, Missouri have established relationships with people and gotten them to church. Then after the person has heard the Gospel and walked an aisle where he received Christ, this person is more likely to get involved in the church and grow in Christ. But neither one emphasis excludes the other because some who receive Christ at the front door come to church and some who walk an aisle and pray the sinner's prayer, never return to church.

The church-planter faces the alternative of building his church on door-knocking (evangelism) or on ministering to mature Christians. The answer is in neither extreme but in a combination of the ehthusiasm of young Christians and the maturity of the old. But with this combination, never forget evangelism. The purpose of a church is winning the lost to Jesus Christ. The young church, like the old churches, can lose their candlestick when they lose their soul-winning perspective of evangelism.

76. <u>Train personal soul winners</u>. Set up a schedule and train people at a definite time each week. Actually take them on soul-winning visitation. Continually enlist new people to be trained. A pastor should keep multiplying himself by training others to help him evangelize.

77. <u>Use authorities for credibility to the new church</u>. The author told Carl Godwin when he went to Lincoln that he should have authorities to speak to his people; these men would expand the vision of his people, as well as

substantiate his ministry. The people of Lincoln had never heard of a super-aggressive church that attempted to reach an entire city. They had always thought in terms of a local neighborhood parish church, the typical American view of Christianity.

Dr. Greg Dixon of Indianapolis Baptist Temple said that when his church was young and struggling, he had Dr. John Rawlings come and preach for him. It gave young Dixon credibility in the eyes of the congregation and it gave the young church credibility in the community's eyes. The church planter should attempt to schedule the following for his church.

> 1. Pastors of large recognized churches.
> 2. Educators of recognized schools.
> 3. Musicians.
> 4. College musical groups.

78. <u>Use radio</u>. A number of church planters have used the traditional radio programs to reach people with some success but high media costs have forced some to consider spot announcements. Radio and television spots have worked in Salem. A number of people first attended the church because of one-minute commercials on local television or radio. Rudy Holland states, "We believe in using every available means to get people to come under the sound of the gospel. We stress a people-centered, not a program-centered gospel.

In the fall of 1981, Russ Merrin reached central Long Island, New York by radio spots and a weekly radio program. Whereas most denominational churches are started as neighborhood churches, the super aggressive church wants to reach the entire area, so he gets on the radio and has the potential of reaching everyone.

79. <u>Plan a charter/organizational service</u>. After the church has about twelve to twenty-four members, plan for the organizational service. Most church planters will invite the pastor from a sponsoring church or a respected pastor to officiate at the chartering service. Other fundamental churches in the area, plus pastors from churches giving financial support should be invited. See the chapter on theology of chartering a church.

80. <u>Support missions</u>. The field is the world, not just the area where the new church is located. As soon as possible, the new church should begin supporting missions. Most new churches should support at least one foreign missionary and at least one other church that is younger than they are.

81. <u>Wait for deacons</u>. The author tells new churches to wait at least one year before electing deacons. He has seen young churches crippled by deacons who try to control the church planter. Many deacons come from other churches where they have been taught that deacons ran the church. By waiting for one year the church planter has time to teach the young church the biblical role of deacons and pastors. Also, there are other reasons why the author tells the new church not to elect deacons for at least one year.

> 1. The first deacons (Acts 6) were appointed approximately one year after the church began.
> 2. "Lay hands suddenly on no man" means a work is hurt when immature leaders are elevated without training and experience.
> 3. Let every man in the new church act in the role of a deacon until those who are evidently appointed by God distinguish themselves by their service.

Al Henson suggests a new church should not elect deacons until it has grown to the size of the church in Acts 6 (about 50,000 people). The author agrees a new church should wait for deacons but suggests the church wait a year. Time is needed to fully know people and allow leadership to arise.

82. <u>Find land for a permanent location</u>. Choose a permanent location as soon as possible. It may not be possible to complete this step before starting the church, but the general area should be decided on by then. Certain principles are important to remember. Jim Singleton spent many hours looking for the correct location. It had to be: (1) easily accessible; (2) centrally located to the three cities (Tempe, Mesa, and Chandler--that's why it's called Tri-City); (3) not chosen because the ground was inexpensive or in an undesirable location; (4) at least ten acres; and (5) near a residential area where people were living, not out in the desert. Singleton prayed over a map and looked at every available property. He announced that the property had to be within one mile of Price and Southern Road. A member phoned to suggest the property on Price and Southern.

The permanent location of the church is highly important. Many young pastors have failed to realize the value of a good location. With the pressure of limited funds, they have settled for less expensive, out-of-the-way locations. The church-planter should drive through the neighborhood and take note of: (1) the public schools, (2) the shopping centers, (3) the existing churches, (4) the price and value of homes, (5) the projection of new homes, (6) the size of building lots, (7) the topography, (8) water, sewerage and gas connections, (9) industrial and other barriers on the neighborhood, and (10) the main arteries and thoroughfares.

The church-planter should get the zoning ordinances in a city to determine restrictions on his proposed church. Some require a large paved parking lot with a low ratio of parking spaces to auditorium size; and others have no such restrictions. In a day of mobility, if zoning restrictions are severe, the pastor should look to the next municipality that is more conducive to building a church.

> Four Criteria for a Good Church Site
> 1. Accessibility
> 2. Visibility
> 3. Relationship to the neighborhood
> 4. Adequacy

Accessibility. Accessibility means members have quick and easy access to the church site. Most of the members will travel by car except for those who come by the church bus. Very few will walk to service. In our day of mobility, people will go as far to church as they drive to work. Some drive 20 miles one way to earn their paycheck. Hence, it is possible for a man to drive long distances to church. Studies have found that a man will drive 20 miles to church if it is located on the expressway. However, the same man would not drive five miles across the city in stop-and-go traffic, thinking that distance is too far. In Los Angeles, people tend to judge distances by time rather than miles. Five minutes on the expressway is not as prohibitive as 15 minutes through traffic, even though it is half the distance.

Accessibility also means locating where the largest number of people are living. The people must have access to the church, but the church must also have access to the people. Sometimes, the young church will have to buy property on the edge of the city before private homes are built. Hence, their members will have to drive out to the church. However, the church will be located in the middle of housing projects within five to ten years.

Whereas, ten years ago experts were counseling against locating on heavily traveled highways because of the danger to children, most church-planters now maintain that a major artery is an excellent site. The danger to those who walk to Sunday School has disappeared. Of course, this principle applies to the United States, not other countries where a vast majority of the population walks to church.

Visibility. The church should be visible to the neighborhood it desires to serve. If at all possible, place the building on a slight elevation so it can be seen from the street with the most traffic. Many churches have used signs to attract attention, but studies show that the public remembers the building better than any other form of media.

Before purchasing the site, check the zoning to make sure that no tall buildings or industry can be located next to the church. Not only would they hide the church from view, its image would be destroyed in the community. For some reason, Americans have a subconscious expectation that a church should be located in a residential neighborhood, not an industrial area.

One has even testified that a conspicuous site is worth more to a local church than a full-page advertisement in the newspaper every day of the year. This claim is probably exaggerated, but does support the argument for a good location.

Relationship to the neighborhood plan. The church should be located near the focal point of the neighborhood. Hence, residents pass it each day on their way to shop or work. If it is possible, locate the building near a shopping center so that the parking lot serves a dual purpose. Unfortunately, property near a shopping center is usually too expensive for a church.

A location near an elementary or high school is sometimes a focal point in the community. Here, a church has accessibility and visibility. Also, it is near people, its point of ministry.

Adequacy. The church site must be adequate to complete its entire program. Whereas, a few years ago churches were buying four or five acres, now young men are looking for ten acres or more. Some have even purchased a church campus of 100 acres. A building site may be attractive, but when considering a complete program, it may be far too small. If a pastor-planter has a great vision, he will need a larger amount of space to carry out his ministry. Space is needed for parking, driveways, buildings, walkways, and expansion. Rudy Holland maintains, "Never consider less than ten acres for a new church site. I suggest seeking land on a major highway or city thoroughfare. God's work deserves the best location in town." Berean Baptist Church is on 11.482 acres of land, centered

Notes

7/8 mile from Interstate 81 on Exit 41. This is four blocks north of Highway 460, on City Bypass 419. Holland believes his location is an important factor in his church growth.

Check the master plan of the city to see if a future freeway or highway expansion will divide or partition part of your ground. Also, check other regulations such as setback requirements, flood planes, and amount of parking that will be allowed in the future. Some cities have not allowed churches to build on large acreages because the property would be tax free. Some city fathers feeling that they need tax income will not zone a large acreage for a church campus.

If the site does not already have water, sewerage, and gas connections, the expense should be added in the total site cost. If a well must be driven or sewer lines constructed, the cost may be excessive. In some areas a church may have to install septic tanks; for commercial use they must be large and expensive. Some churches have had to build complete sewerage installation plants costing over $100,000.00.

A new pastor should find an acreage almost immediately and place a down payment on the property (unless an abandoned church building is available). The fact of owning property will give cohesiveness and permanence to a young congregation. As soon as new property is secured, place a sign, "Future Home of _____ Church." This will give the responsibility of ownership to your people and advertise your existence to the community.

83. <u>Build as soon as possible.</u>

The acquisition of buildings and property is more important in American church growth than at other times in past history. In the early church, Christians met on Solomon's porch for preaching and fellowship. Also, they met in private homes, in the school of Tyrannus, in open amphitheaters and caves. There has always been some central focal place for assembly. Since the first century of Christianity, Christians have constructed buildings. In our century, God has used many unusual locations to establish local churches. A boat house in Garland, Texas launched the LaVonne Drive Baptist Church. The Central Baptist Church in Phoenix, Arizona first met around picnic tables in a park. Trinity Baptist Church in Chattanooga, Tennessee was begun in a carport, and Calvary Baptist Church in Ft. Lauderdale, Florida was begun in a display home. In addition to these, churches have been begun in feed stores, fire departments, abandoned grocery stores, lodge halls, funeral homes, bankrupt soft drink bottling plants and other buildings that brought a young congregation out of the elements. As temporary as these permanent buildings were, an element of stability was added when a congregation moved into its own building.

Some advocate that a church should remain in rented facilities, not investing its money in buildings. One pastor desired to remain in a rented public school; the congregation was too poor to buy property and construct a building. To this day, they are still too poor and remain in the rented school. They argue that too much money is diverted from missions. As valid as this argument is, the church will have more in the future to give to missions by following prescribed methods of growth.

Church planters realize what moving into their own building can do to strengthen a young church. Rudy Holland in Roanoke, Virginia indicated many families remained on the fringe, watching the young church as it met in the rented facilities of the civic center. But when it moved into its own facilities, the attitude of Christians on the outside changed. Families began joining. These families brought financial strength, teaching abilities and maturity with them. Holland explains, "Do not criticize these people for lack of pioneering zeal. They had an honest doubt. When we bought property and built, they knew we were not a flash in the pan."

When a congregation moves into its own facilities, it gains the following advantage: (1) the community realizes the church is permanent, no longer a transient group; (2) the young congregation becomes a part of the city, a property holder; (3) the young congregation identifies with the neighborhood, they belong to the landscape and the community; (4) permanent facilities allow people to funnel their energies into other ministry rather than preparing the building each week. One pastor indicated each week he had to set up chairs, distribute hymnbooks, and get the building ready for a meeting. Jim Mastin at Milwaukee indicated each Saturday night he labored until 2 or 3 a.m., getting the building ready for Sunday services. Many times they had to sweep up the cigarette butts and take out the beer cans before holding church in the YMCA. He complained, "Our teachers could not hang a picture and did not use as many visual aids because they had to drag flannel boards in and take down pictures after each class."

When interviewing the pastors of the ten largest Sunday Schools, most reiterated, "Never get out of a building campaign." By this, they meant a church should always plan another building for added growth. Christianity is a process, not a product. Therefore, the young congregation should always be building additional rooms or enlarging the auditorium. Physical expansion reflects spiritual growth and, if a church is winning souls, they will need more space to teach and preach. Also, when the neighborhood sees additions being built, they realize the church is growing.

Notes

Even though the building only houses the meetings of the church, Americans still judge a church by its buildings. Sloppily kept buildings indicate a messy attitude toward Christianity. When a congregation will sacrifice to build an auditorium, they tell the community that preaching is important.

84. <u>Get financing for growth</u>. An independent Baptist church does not have a central loan fund such as found in denominations. Yet the church needs financing for property, buildings and equipment. If the church waits until it can pay cash for these items, it will mortgage its mission to "slow growth mentality." Most lending institutions will not loan them much, if any at all. The following is a series of financial steps that are possible in the early 80's.

a. Purchase land with the owner holding a note for the church. The cash in the building fund should equal for ten percent to twenty-five percent down payment. Put as much money into the land as this is the only equity the young church has.

b. Raise a percentage of the building cost and borrow the remainder, using the property as collateral. Landscaping, painting and some other contracting jobs can be done by the congregation, making the difference between the cost of the building and the percent that a lending institution will give to a young church.

The Berean Baptist Church in Roanoke financed its four buildings by issuing church bonds. This is one method for financing a new church, inasmuch as most banks will not loan to new congregations. Usually, the most important factor in the issuance of church bonds is working with a qualified, reputable bond company. Some churches end up in trouble with bond programs because they deal with bond companies that are only interested in making profit.

In reference to bond programs, the pastor should acquaint himself with the state laws regarding church bonds. Obtain a good general knowledge of the strengths and weaknesses of church bonds before trying to sell your people on the program. The bond program success rests largely upon the pastor. Never make the purchase of a church bond sound like a charitable donation. The public is lending you its money.

The size of the bond issue will differ in each church according to income, mortgage value, growth pattern, and operating expenses.

Questions for Review

1. The church planter should begin the preparation work for a new church as soon as he arrives on the field. True False

2. These eighty-four steps formulate the perfect strategy for church planting in America. True False

3. The church planter must have a clear idea of his church before he arrives in the city to which God calls him. True False

4. The vision of what God will do in your city will come from other more mature pastors. True False

5. God leads some men into church planting and calls others into established pastorates. True False

6. The call of God will prevent the church planter from becoming discouraged with the work. True False

7. The burden for church planting is an internal pressure that comes to the church planter. True False

8. The desire to start a church will excite a man for an area, every time he thinks about the town. True False

9. The church planter should see fruit (i.e. souls saved) when he starts the church as evidence of his call. True False

10. Pastor Younge Chou advises church planters to fast before starting a church. True False

11. The church planter's wife will be an important part of the ministry in a new church. True False

12. A growing church should have a positive biblical message. True False

13. A church planter should depend on printed sermon outlines during the first year until he has others visiting and can spend more time preparing his own sermons. True False

14. The church planter should save his best sermons for later when the church is larger. True False

15. The most crucial doctrine for the church planter to know is inerrancy. True False

16. The church is an assembly of believers organized for evangelism, education, worship and fellowship, the administering of the ordinances and reflecting of spiritual gifts. True False

17. New churches often split over issues of ecclesiology. True False

18. Men in fundamental schools are good at church planting because they learn a philosophy from the pastor of their home church or the leader of their school. True False

19. The church planter should prepare only short range goals during his first year. True False

20. A man who is called to start a church can consider starting in any city to which his pastor sends him. True False

21. It is best for the church planter to work part time to help out with finances until the church is established. True False

22. Eliezer was commissioned to start a church by Abraham. True False

23. The principles by which God calls a man to full time service are similar to the principles by which He directs a man to a specific city. True False

24. The place to begin a church is usually the place of greatest need. True False

25. There is no town in America that is over saturated with the gospel. True False

26. The church planter should survey the community as soon as he moves to town. True False

27. The church planter should strive for economy when looking for a meeting place. True False

28. A hotel conference room is a good place to start a church. True False

29. Sophistication and revivalism cannot be mixed. True False

30. Bill Monroe posted motivational posters around his office. True False

31. Everything rises or falls on leadership. True False

32. If men are available, it is best to establish an advisory board until deacons are elected. True False

33. The ministry is one of the easiest places to backslide. — True False

34. The secret to getting 1,000 in church is through Sunday School promotions. — True False

35. The pastor/planter should begin to enforce standards for workers after he has enough people to choose from especially if some get mad and leave the church. — True False

36. Greatness in the ministry is developed by associating with and learning from great men. — True False

37. The church planter should have an older pastor who will counsel him as he starts the church. — True False

38. Bill Munroe manages the finances of his church following the principles of management by assets. — True False

39. Financing by cash flow dictates that a church must have more cash income than outgo. — True False

40. Receiving a number of special offerings each month helps teach good stewardship to members of a new church. — True False

41. The church planter/pastor should be careful not to let financial details become public. — True False

42. A church should begin to get an annual audit as soon as income reaches two hundred thousand dollars annually or at the start of a Christian school. — True False

43. A pastor should give priority to financial advice from other pastors more often than from an unsaved accountant. — True False

44. It is best to get a church member who is a CPA to audit your books and save money. — True False

45. July is the best month for a stewardship campaign because the church calendar is not busy and some churches start and end their fiscal year June 30. — True False

46. The pastor/planter should expect people to tithe from the beginning of the church. — True False

47. People who support a ministry financially are more loyal to the church in other areas. — True False

48. A new church should invest in good financial records.	True	False
49. A church planter should raise money to operate four weeks before starting the church.	True	False
50. A church planter should hire qualified people to survey the town.	True	False
51. Government offices provide some necessary information to survey the town.	True	False
52. Jews would not begin a synagogue with less than twelve families in biblical times.	True	False
53. An established neighborhood is a better place to start a church than a transient neighborhood.	True	False
54. Jesus taught the idea of evangelizing in an area most conducive to the gospel.	True	False
55. The church congregation should choose a name for their church at the chartering service.	True	False
56. The pastor should open a post office box immediately after organizing the church.	True	False
57. Promotional pictures of the pastor and his family should be ready before starting the church.	True	False
58. The post office will explain details regarding a nonprofit permit number.	True	False
59. It is best for the church planter to establish his home in town before holding services.	True	False
60. The church planter should never sign checks.	True	False
61. The church planter should begin receiving money six weeks after he arrives on the field.	True	False
62. Some of the greatest expenses in starting the church occur in the first months.	True	False
63. All gifts should be receipted by the church.	True	False

64. The pastor should not prepare a budget until the end of the first month and he knows how much income he can expect. True False

65. The pastor/planter should be familiar with tax laws when planning his budget. True False

66. The pastor/planter should raise financial support like a foreign missionary. True False

67. A new church should be incorporated after six months. True False

68. Prospects for a new church can be found among friends of the church planter in the area. True False

69. The pastor must complete forms if he does not want to participate in the Social Security program. True False

70. A prospect is any one who does not attend your church but should and could attend. True False

71. The pastor and charter members should prepare a constitution at least one month before the charter service. True False

72. The first location should be as near the permanent location as possible. True False

73. Direct mail is too expensive to be considered by most new churches. True False

74. Established churches will often loan or give hymn books to a new church. True False

75. One of the churches first purchases should be an offset printing press. True False

76. Saturation evangelism is using every available means to reach every available person at every available time. True False

77. The pastor/planter should set financial goals but not evangelism goals. True False

78. The church becomes a part of the community when its offerings cover all weekly expenses. True False

79. The use of logos and slogans in church advertising tends to cast negative attitudes on a church. True False

80. A large sandwich board makes a good sign for use on temporary facilities. True False

81. The church sign is best located inside the building rather than outside. True False

82. The first church brochure should strive to show credibility for the new church. True False

83. Door to door visitation remains a necessity in starting a new church. True False

84. The pastor should plan to do all the visiting himself until he has trained soul winners. True False

85. Get acquainted meetings are best held when the new church is organized. True False

86. Mature Christians in dead churches may be reached through get acquainted meetings. True False

87. The church should hold a Wednesday evening prayer meeting for about one month before starting Sunday services. True False

88. Newspaper advertising for a new church should begin advertising the first service. True False

89. Free advertising usually does not produce results. True False

90. Church planters are rarely criticized by pastors of fundamental churches, only liberal ministers. True False

91. The pastor should be proud of his church from its small beginnings. True False

92. It is important that new church members should see both victories and failures to accurately appraise the ministry. True False

93. Country music should be the chief style of gospel music used in a new church because of its popular appeal. True False

94. Church services should be well planned but not liturgical. True False

95. Offerings should become a regular part of the church service as soon as it is chartered. True False

96. People should be reminded of the need when an offering is received. True False

97. The use of offering envelopes aids in the taking of an offering. — True False

98. The Sunday School should begin with five classes. — True False

99. Visitors should be followed up by letter. — True False

100. Doctrinal distinctives should be taught from the beginning. — True False

101. Since staff members might split a new church, the church planter should not hire staff members for at least eighteen months. — True False

102. A church should receive an offering for a building fund at the organizational meeting. — True False

103. A new church should balance different evangelism strategies in their visitation program. — True False

104. The best way to train soul winners in a new church is through classroom instruction. — True False

105. The new church should not invite guest speakers in because the people will not identify with the pastor's preaching. — True False

106. Pastors of large churches and educators affiliated with recognized schools are good men to use to bring credibility to a new church. — True False

107. Spot advertising on radio is effective in reaching large areas. — True False

108. It is usually best for the church planter to charter his new church. — True False

109. The church should support foreign missions about two years after starting. — True False

110. Deacons should be elected at the charter service because their office is taught in the Scripture. — True False

111. A church should find a permanent location as soon as possible. — True False

112. A location should be chosen where the church is easily accessible and visible to passing traffic. — True False

113. When buying land, the church will normally want at least ten acres. — True False

114. If possible, the church should remain in rented facilities as long as possible to save money. — True False

SECTION IV

APPENDIX

This section includes some tools the church planter will need to plant a new church. First, he will need a church constitution that is fundamental in doctrine, congregational in authority and pastoral leadership in administration (see Chapter 14). This church constitution included the historic doctrinal statement that is taken from the New Hampshire Confession of Faith that is over 200 years old. Next, the church planter will need an organizing instrument. The one included in Chapter 15 has been used by Baptists for almost 200 years to incorporate churches. Chapter 16 is a Community Survey that can be used by the church planter to gather information from the area where he is considering starting a church. Chapter 17 is information on the Liberty Baptist Fellowship for Church Planting and an application that must be filed with their office to receive financial support.

CHAPTER 14

CONSTITUTION

Constitution of Oakland Heights Baptist Church of Oakville, Ontario

Preamble

We, the members of Oakland Heights Baptist Church, in orderly manner do hereby establish the following principles by which we mutually agree to be governed in the affairs of our church.

Article I: Name

This church shall be known as the Oakland Heights Baptist Church of Oakville, Ontario.

Article II: Purpose

This church shall have as its purpose the evangelism of the lost, the promotion of the historic Baptist faith, the worship of God, the education of its members, friends, and their families, and such other purposes as are specified in the Holy Bible for a New Testament church.

Article III: Statement of Faith

This church holds the following Statement of Faith as being a summary of Christian doctrine whose authority consists only in its agreement with the Word of God.

I. OF THE SCRIPTURES

We believe that the Holy Bible was written by men supernaturally inspired; that it has truth without any admixture of error for its matter; and therefore is, and shall remain to the end of the age, the only complete and final revelation of the will of God to man; the true center of Christian union and the supreme standard by which all human conduct, creeds and opinions should be tried.

1. By "The Holy Bible" we mean that collection of sixty-six books, from Genesis to Revelation, which, as originally written does not only contain and convey the Word of God but IS the very Word of God.

2. By "Inspiration" we mean that the books of the Bible were written by holy men of old, as they were moved by the Holy Spirit, in such a definite way that their writings were supernaturally and verbally inspired and free from error, as no other writings have ever been or ever will be inspired.

II. THE TRUE GOD

We believe that there is one, and only one, living and true God, an infinite intelligent Spirit, the Maker and Supreme Ruler of heaven and earth; inexpressibly glorious in holiness, and worthy of all possible honor, confidence and love; that in the unity of the Godhead there are three persons, the Father, the Son and the Holy Ghost, equal in every divine perfection, and executing distinct but harmonious offices in the great work of redemption.

III. THE HOLY SPIRIT

We believe that the Holy Spirit is a divine person; equal with God the Father and God the Son and of the same nature; that He was active in the creation, and in His relation to the unbelieving world He restrains the evil one until God's purpose is fulfilled; for He convicts of sin, of judgment and of righteousness; that He bears witness to the Truth of the Gospel in preaching and testimony; that He is the agent in the New Birth; that He seals, endues, guides, teaches, witnesses, sanctifies and helps the believer.

IV. OF THE DEVIL OR SATAN

We believe that Satan was once holy, and enjoyed heavenly honors; but through pride and ambition to be as the Almighty, fell and drew after him a host of angels, that he is now the malignant prince of the power of the air, and the unholy god of this world. We hold him to be man's great tempter, the enemy of God and His Christ, the accuser of the saints, the author of all false religions, the chief power back of the present apostasy; the lord of the Antichrist, and the author of all the powers of darkness-- destined however to final defeat at the hands of God's Son, and the judgment of an eternal justice in hell, a place prepared for him and his angels.

V. OF THE CREATION

We believe in the Genesis account of creation, and that it is to be accepted literally, and not allegorically or figuratively; that man was created directly in God's own image and after his own likeness; that man's creation was not a matter of evolution or evolutionary change of species, or developments through interminable periods of time from lower to higher forms; that all animals and vegetable life were made directly, and God's established law was that they should bring forth only "after their kind."

VI. OF THE FALL OF MAN

We believe that man was created in innocence under the law of his Maker, but by voluntary transgression fell from his sinless and happy state, in consequence of which, all mankind are now sinners, not by constraint, but by choice; and therefore under just condemnation without defense or excuse.

VII. OF THE VIRGIN BIRTH

We believe that Jesus Christ was begotten of the Holy Ghost in a miraculous manner; born of Mary, a virgin, as no other man was ever born or can ever be born of woman, and He is both the Son of God, and God the Son.

VIII. OF THE ATONEMENT FOR SIN

We believe that the salvation of sinners is wholly of grace; through the mediatorial offices of the Son of God, who by the appointment of the Father, freely took upon Him our nature, yet without sin, honored the divine law by His personal obedience, and by His death made a full and vicarious atonement for our sins; that His atonement consisted not in setting us an example by His death as a martyr, but was the voluntary substitution of Himself in the sinner's place, the just dying for the unjust, Christ the Lord, bearing our sins in His own body on the tree; that, having risen from the dead, He is now enthroned in heaven and uniting in His wonderful person the tenderest sympathies with divine perfection. He is every way qualified to be a suitable, a compassionate and an all-sufficient Saviour.

IX. OF GRACE IN THE NEW CREATION

We believe that in order to be saved, sinners must be born again; that the new birth is a new creation in Jesus Christ; that it is instantaneous and not a process; that in the new birth the one dead in trespasses and in sins is made a partaker of the divine nature and receives eternal life, the free gift of God; that the new creation is brought about in a manner above our comprehension, not by culture, not by character, nor by the will of man, but wholly and solely by the power of the Holy Spirit in connection with divine truth, so as to secure our voluntary obedience to the Gospel; that its proper evidence appears in the holy fruits of repentance and faith and newness of life.

X. OF THE FREENESS OF SALVATION

We believe in God's electing grace; that the blessings of salvation are made free to all by the Gospel; that it is the immediate duty of all to accept them by a cordial, penitent and obedient faith; and that nothing prevents the salvation of the greatest sinner on earth but his own inherent depravity and voluntary rejection of the Gospel; which rejection involves him in an aggravated condemnation.

XI. OF JUSTIFICATION

We believe that the great Gospel which Christ secures to such as believe in Him is justification; that justification includes the pardon of sin, and the gift of eternal life on principles of righteousness; that it is bestowed not in consideration of any works or righteousness which we have done; but solely through faith in the Redeemer's blood, His righteousness is imputed unto us.

XII. OF REPENTANCE AND FAITH

We believe that repentance and faith are solemn obligations; and also inseparable graces, wrought in our souls by the quickening Spirit of God; thereby, being deeply convicted of our guilt, danger and helplessness, and of the way of Salvation by Christ, we turn to God with unfeigned contrition, confession and supplication for mercy; at the same time heartily receiving the Lord Jesus Christ and openly confessing Him as our only and all-sufficient Saviour.

XIII. OF THE CHURCH

We believe that a church of Christ is a congregation of baptized believers associated by a covenant of faith and fellowship of the Gospel; observing the ordinances of Christ; governed by His laws; and exercising the gifts, rights, and privileges invested in them by His Word; that its officers of ordination are pastors or elders and deacons, whose qualifications, claims and duties are clearly defined in the Scriptures; we believe the true mission of the church is found in the Great Commission: first, to make individual disciples; second, to build up the church; third, to teach and instruct as He commanded. We do not believe in the reversal of this order; we hold that the local church has the absolute right of self government, free from the interference of any hierarchy of individuals or organizations; and that the one and only superintendent is Christ through the Holy Spirit; that it is scriptural for true churches to cooperate with each other in contending for the faith and for the furtherance of the Gospel; that every church is the sole and only judge of the measure and method of its cooperation; on all matters of membership, of policy, of government, of discipline, of benevolence, the will of the local church is final.

XIV. OF BAPTISM AND THE LORD'S SUPPER

We believe that Christian baptism is the immersion in water of a believer; in the name of the Father, of the Son, and of the Holy Ghost, with the authority of the local church, to show forth in a solemn and beautiful emblem our faith in the crucified, buried and risen Saviour, with its effect in our death to sin and resurrection to a new life; that it is prerequisite to the privileges of a church relation and to the Lord's Supper; in which the members of the church by the sacred use of bread and wine are to commemorate together the dying love of Christ, preceded always by solemn self-examination.

XV. OF THE PERSEVERANCE OF THE SAINTS

We believe that such only are real believers as endure unto the end; that their persevering attachment to Christ is the grand mark which distinguishes them from superficial professors, that a special Providence watches over their welfare; and that they are kept by the power of God through faith unto eternal salvation.

XVI. OF THE RIGHTEOUS AND THE WICKED

We believe that there is a radical and essential difference between the righteous and the wicked; that such only as through faith are justified in the name of the Lord Jesus, and sanctified by the Spirit of our God, are truly righteous in His esteem; while all such as continue in impenitence and unbelief are in His sight wicked, and under the curse, and this distinction holds among men both in and after death, in the everlasting felicity of the saved and the everlasting conscious suffering of the lost.

XVII. OF CIVIL GOVERNMENT

We believe that civil government is of divine appointment, for the interests and good order of human society; that magistrates are to be prayed for; conscientiously honored and obeyed; except only in things opposed to the will of our Lord Jesus Christ; who is the only Lord of the conscience, and the coming Prince of the kings of earth.

XVIII. OF THE RESURRECTION AND RETURN OF CHRIST AND RELATED EVENTS

We believe in and accept the sacred Scriptures upon these subjects at their face and full value. Of the resurrection, we believe that Christ arose bodily "the third day according to the Scriptures;" that He ascended "to the right hand of the throne of God," that He alone is our "merciful and faithful high priest in things pertaining to God;" "That this same Jesus which is taken up from you into heaven shall so come in like manner as ye have seen Him to into heaven"--bodily, personally and visibly; that the "dead in Christ shall rise first;" that the living saints "shall be changed in a moment, in the twinkling of an eye, at the last trump;" "that the Lord God shall give unto Him the throne of His Father David;" and that "Christ shall reign a thousand years in righteousness until he hath put all enemies under His feet."

XIX. OF MISSIONS

We believe that the command to give the Gospel to the world is clear and unmistakable and this commission was given to the churches.

XX. OF THE GRACE OF GIVING

We believe that God's method of financing His earthly work of spreading the Gospel to all nations; the care of the churches and the support of the ministry is by the tithes and offerings of His people. That it is to be given to the Lord through His chruch or storehouse to be distributed as directed by the leadership of the Spirit as the need arises. The time to tithe is upon the first day of the week. That everyone is accountable to the Lord for one-tenth of his income and that tithing was instituted long before the law was ever given and was practiced by the early church.

Article IV: Covenant

As a bond of unity among us Oakland Heights Baptist Church accepts for its member the following covenant.

Having been led by the Holy Spirit to receive the Lord Jesus Christ as our Saviour and on profession of our faith in Him, having been baptized in the name of the Father, and of the Son, and of the Holy Spirit, we do now most solemnly and joyfully enter into covenant with one another as one body in Christ.

We promise that we will watch over and counsel one another in the spirit of brotherly love, that we will remember one another in our prayers, and that we will aid each other in sickness and distress.

We further agree, by the aid of the Holy Spirit, to walk together in Christian love; to strive for the advancement of this church in knowledge, holiness, and comfort; to promote its prosperity and spirituality; to sustain its worship, ordinances, discipline, and doctrines; to give it a sacred preeminence over all institutions of human origin; and to contribute cheerfully and regularly to the support of the ministry, the expenses of the church, the relief of the poor, and the spread of the Gospel through all nations.

We further covenant to maintain family and private devotion; to religiously educate our children; to seek the salvation of our kindred and acquaintances; to live carefully in this present world; to be just in our dealings, faithful in our engagements, and exemplary in our deportment; to avoid all tattling, backbiting, and excessive anger; to abstain from everything that will cause our brother to stumble or that will bring reproach upon the cause of Christ; and to strive to grow in the grace and knowledge of our Lord and Saviour, that amidst evil and good report we will humbly and earnestly seek to live to the honor and glory of Him who loved us and gave Himself for us.

We moreover engage that when we remove from this place we will, as soon as possible, unite with some other church where we can carry out the spirit of this covenant and the principles of God's Word.

Article V: Church Membership

The membership of this church shall consist of persons who have accepted Jesus Christ as personal Saviour and have been baptized by immersion into this church or a church of like faith and order. The membership reserves the exclusive right to determine who shall be a member. New members may be accepted by vote of the membership when requesting membership in any of the following ways: (1) by profession of faith and baptism, (2) by letter from a church of like-faith and order, (3) by statement of faith, having been scripturally baptized by another church of like-faith and order, or (4) by restoration. Membership can be terminated by (1) death, (2) dismission to a church of like-faith and order, (3) discipline, or (4) the request of the members.

Article VI: Church Officers

1. Pastor: The pastor is the undershepherd of Jesus Christ, the leader of the church, and is primarily responsible to Christ for the work of the church. He is the chief executive and administrative officer of the church in spiritual and physical matters. The pastor is to be called to the church to serve indefinitely.

When the church becomes without a pastor the deacons will serve as a pulpit committee to seek out a new pastor. They shall prayerfully search until agreed on one candidate to recommend to the church. The church will be given the opportunity to vote within one week of the deacons' recommendations to call the candidate as pastor. A two-thirds majority vote is required to call a pastor.

The pastor may be removed from office at a special business meeting of the congregation called by the deacons where reasons for his removal would be presented; he would be allowed to answer the accusations, and a vote taken. The pastor should be notified of the meeting and of the charges to be brought against him before notice of the meeting is given to the congregation. A two-thirds majority vote would be required to remove the pastor. This step should be taken very carefully and prayerfully.

2. Church Staff: The pastor may bring in such staff as he feels are necessary to assist him in providing for the church. They will be employed at a salary agreed to by the trustees and work under the direct supervision of the pastor, or indirectly under him and directly under the supervision of a staff member appointed by the pastor.

3. Deacons: Deacons are to advise and assist the pastor in the spiritual interests of the church; seek out, visit, and minister to the physical, moral, and spiritual needs of the sick, aged, and necessities among the membership; review the church membership at least once a year and inquire as to the regularity and faithfulness of the members in attendance and support of the church; serve at the Lord's Supper Table; and be zealous to guard and to promote a spirit of unity and peace within the church. They will act as a sounding board from the congregation to the pastor and shall discuss matters of importance to the church.

Deacons are to meet the spiritual qualifications given in 1 Timothy 3:8-13 and Acts 6:1-6.

The first deacons will be recommended to the church by the pastor, thereafter the deacons shall recommend to the church names of those to be added. The church shall vote on each name presented.

4. Trustees: The trustees will hold in trust the church property, serve as a financial advisory committee for the pastor, and maintain the church insurance program. Trustees have no power to buy, sell, mortgage, lease, or transfer any property without a specific vote of the church authorizing each action. They shall sign legal papers as needed and directed by the church. They shall be elected permanently by the church.

5. Treasurer: The treasurer shall see that accurate records are maintained of all receipts and disbursements and the giving of individual contributions. The treasurer will be one of the co-signers on the checks. The budget shall be prepared under the supervision of the pastor in assistance by the treasurer and a financial committee if elected. The budget is then approved by the congregation at the annual meeting. The treasurer is responsible for the investment of the funds for the ministry of the church. All disbursements are to be made according to the budget as approved by the church. The treasurer is to provide a monthly financial report to the church. The treasurer is to be appointed by the pastor subject to approval by the deacons and trustees.

6. Others: Other officers of the church and/or its related ministries may be elected or appointed as they are needed.

7. Standards for Leaders: All elected or appointed leaders of this church and/or any of its related ministries shall be saved, active members of the church in agreement with the doctrinal position of the church, tithers, soul winners, loyal to the pastor, and living a separated Christian life.

Article VII: Church Meetings

   1. For Worship and Study. The church shall have regular services or Sundays and a midweek meeting, plus such meetings of organizations as they are needed. Special meetings as revivals, conferences, music programs, and such will also be held from time to time as the pastor sees need.

   2. For Business: The church shall meet for an annual business meeting in January. This meeting shall report to the church the activities of the previous year and include the election of officers and any other business to be presented to the church. In addition special meetings may be called by the pastor and/or deacons with seven days notice to the church. The purpose of the special meeting must be announced. A majority of those present and qualified to vote may conduct any church business, except as where otherwise qualified by this constitution.

Article VIII: Church Government

   Each member of the church will have an equal voice in its government, exercised through a vote at regular or called business meetings. The pastor shall serve as moderator of all business meetings. If the church is without a pastor, the chairman of the deacons will serve as moderator. The church shall vote on the pastor, deacons and trustees; establishment or modification of major policies; the buying, selling or mortgaging of church properties; and the annual church budget. Meetings are to be conducted in accordance with Roberts Rules of Order. Matters of lesser importance will be handled by the pastor and staff, deacons, and trustees within their prescribed responsibilities.

Article IX: Relation to Other Churches

   This church shall be fully autonomous in the government of its own affairs, exercising and retaining sole and complete control of all property which shall be held in its name by its trustees. Fellowship and cooperation will be sought with all true believers and congregations, but control of this church and/or its property will never be surrendered.

Article X: Church Finances

   The fiscal year shall be from January 1 through December 31. The members shall be expected to give their tithes and offerings through this church. The treasurer shall keep proper records including a record of individual contributions. A budget shall be prepared by the pastor and trustees and approved by the church. Special offerings may be taken up with the approval of the pastor and/or the trustees.

Article XI: Dissolution

   No part of the property or other buildings of this church shall ever inure to the benefit of any donor, member, officer of the church, or any individual. If for any reason the church is dissolved, all assets shall be distributed equally to organizations selected by the church and recognized as religious and charitable in nature by the Internal Revenue Service.

Article XII: Amendments to Constitution

This constitution may be amended by a two-thirds majority vote of the members present at a called business meeting announced for that purpose.

CHAPTER 15

CHARTERING STATEMENT

NAME OF CHURCH   CITY, STATE

IN THE YEAR OF OUR LORD, SEPTEMBER 24, 1973 WE, the undersigned, relying on the guidance of the Holy Spirit and by the signing of our names hereto do agree and covenant with the Lord Jesus Christ and with one another that we do constitute ourselves as Charter Members of the name of the church, city, state.

FURTHER, we, the undersigned, each declare and confess with our faith wholly in the Lord Jesus Christ for salvation by the experience of the new birth that we have been Scripturally baptized and therefore are qualified to become Charter Members.

ALSO, we the undersigned, do believe in those great distinctive principles for which born again Christians have ever stood, namely:

1. The pre-eminence of Christ as our Divine Lord and Master
2. The supreme authority of the Bible and its sufficiency as our only rule of faith and practice
3. The right of private interpretation and the competency of the individual soul in direct approach to God
4. The absolute separation of Church and State
5. The regenerate church membership
6. The beautiful symbolic ordinance of believer's baptism and the Lord's Supper in obedience to the command of Christ
7. The complete independence of the local church and its interdependence in associated fellowship with other churches
8. The solemn obligation of majority rule, guaranteeing equal rights to all and special privileges to none
9. A world-wide program of missionary fervor and evangelism in obedience to the final command of the Lord Jesus Christ
10. The personal, imminent, pre-millennial return of the Lord Jesus Christ.

AND, we, the undersigned, accept the doctrines of the Articles of Faith included herein; and, accept the duties of the Church Covenant included herein; we assemble ourselves together as the name of the church, and adopt for our plan of outreach, government, and service the By-Laws included herein.

_____
Signed

CHAPTER 16

COMMUNITY SURVEY FOR CHURCH PLANTING

1. Name of city _____

2. General history and interesting background of the city.

3. Maps of the city and surrounding communities (attach)
   Secure and attach reports on community survey and planning.

4. Addresses and phone numbers

    a. Dept. of City Planning

    b. Chamber of Commerce

    c. Department of Tourism

    d. Summarize the aspects and plans for growth in the area

5. Population

    a. Ten mile radius _____; Fiftenn mile _____;
       Twenty mile _____.

    b. Population growth

        1) Increasing or decreasing?

        2) 1960 _____; 1970 _____;
           1980 _____; 1985 _____;
           1990 _____.

    c. Population density per square mile _____.

    d. Racial breakdown of population

        1) Trends from previous census and projections

e. Population breakdown on age levels and family types.

f. Population turnover

   1) Percentage of population moving in or out each year.

g. Incoming commuters?

6. Churches

   a. Number and location of churches of each denomination.

   b. Independent Baptist

      1) Location, history, membership, facilities.

c. Any overriding religious influence or projected problem

7. Employment

    a. Level of employment

        1) Trends of employment

    b. Type of employment and percentage breakdown (white and blue collar)

    c. Types of industry

    d. Industrial growth

        1) Increasing or decreasing

8. Land available

    a. Average cost per acre (note different cost in different areas)

    b. Special building codes

    c. Location of available land

    d. Which way is population moving? Industry moving? Future shopping areas?

9. Transportation

    a. Note the major highways, subways, bus routes

10. Schools

    a. Public and private

    b. Any Christian Day Schools in the vicinity

    c. Colleges and universities

11. Media

    a. Newspapers (daily and weeklies)

    b. Radio and television stations

12. Housing

    a. Houses, apartments

        1) Availability, average cost or rent -- low cost; rental

13. Miscellaneous

    a. Banks

    b. Hospitals

    c. Utilities

14. List the general reasons why an independent Baptist church should be planted in the area.

15. List the general problems that will face a new independent Baptist church in the area. Can these problems be overcome?

CHAPTER 17

LIBERTY BAPTIST FELLOWSHIP
FOR CHURCH PLANTING

Dr. Jerry Falwell recently announced the formation of a new organization called Liberty Baptist Fellowship for Church Planting. This organization will be a tool to help reach the goal of beginning 5,000 new churches by the year 2000. Pastors are banding together because many can do more together than any one alone. Their pastors see the Great Commission as the aim of a local church which commands that: first, people be won to Jesus Christ; second, they must be baptized; and finally, they must be taught Christian doctrine (Matthew 28:19,20). Since this aim is best carried out at home and on the foreign field through the establishment of local churches, Liberty Baptist Fellowship is being organized to help our churches establish more churches.

Liberty Baptist Fellowship is not in competition with other groups nor is it a new denomination. Churches that join are not asked to disassociate from their other church relationships. Dr. Falwell indicated that he will encourage all churches to strengthen their ties with other fundamental organizations in the field of foreign missions, Sunday School enrichment, soul winning and moral reform such as Moral Majority.

Liberty Baptist Fellowship is a network of "like-faith and like-practice" churches that will encourage church planting through education, advertisement, and stimulation. This will take the form of seminars, national conferences, a national newspaper and organizational manuals.

The foundational plank in the fellowship platform is, "Churches plant churches," so the fellowship will help churches plant churches. This principle is in opposition to some denominations that believe it is the duty of headquarters to plant churches.

There are many denominations and groups that are interested in church planting. In addition to this, many large churches have been active in church planting.

For 2000 years pioneers have gone to plant independent local churches that have been effective in winning souls to Jesus Christ. Baptist pastors have crisscrossed America to plant independent Baptist churches, many of them have prospered and captured their towns for Christ. As the growth of the independent Baptist churches across America is viewed, some ask, "What can Liberty Baptist Fellowship for Church Planting do for the church planter that has not been done before?"

First of all, it will give direction and impetus to the movement. Dr. Falwell gave a vision to the students of the Liberty Baptist Schools to plant 5,000 new churches before the year 2000 A.D. Anyone who has been on Liberty Mountain knows that the vision of Dr. Falwell usually becomes a reality. He conceives of plans before most people think of them, he challenges people with plans bigger than most can imagine, and projects his plans farther in the future than most will ever live.

1. L.B.F. -- a channel of motivation. One of the basic purposes of L.B.F. is to keep Liberty men and their churches motivated to plant other churches. Hence, the testimony of Al Henson who established Lighthouse Baptist Church in Nashville, Tennessee and plans to start nine more churches can be communicated to present students and others who will follow his example. Liberty Baptist Fellowship will use newspapers, conferences, and every other means to motivate church planting.

2. L.B.F. -- source of strategy. It is always tragic when a young man goes out and begins a church, then fails. Not only has he hurt his own spiritual growth, but he has hurt any other who would try to establish a church in that town. Plus, those who have established a church any place are disheartened by the news of any church still-birth. Therefore, Liberty Baptist Fellowship will attempt to provide a workable strategy for all church planters to humanly prevent, as much as possible, as many failures as possible.

3. L.B.F. -- source of information. There must be a central source for statistics, successes, and warnings of danger. Liberty Baptist Fellowship is dedicated to locating and categorizing the 5,000 new churches that will be started by the end of this decade. This information will include graduates of the Seminary, College, and Institute and graduates of Liberty Home Bible Institute. In addition to graduates, the list will contain former students of the four schools, plus former employees of the ministry in Lynchburg, plus a number of men who have grown up in the church prior to the founding of the College, and others who have been financially supported by Thomas Road Baptist Church over the years. In addition to these, others will want to have a part in church planting and will join Liberty Baptist Fellowship.

4. L.B.F. -- ecclessiastical identification. Many times a young man goes out and begins a church and the community suspects him because they see no human frame of reference. Liberty Baptist Fellowship will provide brochures and tracts on the nature of the church, the role of the pastor, the doctrine of baptism, and other unique positions taken by Liberty men. Recently, one of our graduates had to face three deacons in his office who had come out of Southern Baptist churches. They felt that our graduate was taking too much authority to himself and that the deacons should have more control in the finances of the church. The deacons felt the pastor was too young and was taking too much leadership in the church. They needed literature that described the church practice taught in Scripture. The Liberty Baptist Fellowship needs to produce literature that supports our church polity and objectives.

5. L.B.F. -- a place of fellowship. Liberty Baptist Fellowship is not an attempt to take the place of the Baptist Bible Fellowship or Southwide Baptist Fellowship, or any other fellowship of independent Baptist churches. It is simply another fellowship for pastors who are like-minded in church planting.

The Liberty Baptist Fellowship for Church Planting is not an alumni organization of the Liberty Schools, even though the majority of its members are from Liberty. If it were an alumni association, each of the pastors would wait for the College to organize and raise the support for the Fellowship.

Liberty Baptist Fellowship is not an extension of the Old-Time Gospel Hour. If it were, all the pastors would wait for Jerry Falwell to run the organization, and ultimately pay the bills.

The Liberty Baptist Fellowship has not taken financial support from any outside source because it is a fellowship of Baptist pastors for the purpose of building Baptist churches, operated and supported by Baptist pastors.

It is a fellowship of Baptist pastors, not an association of Baptist churches. No church can join the fellowship, nor can the fellowship control any church. There is no incident in the New Testament where churches were organizationally linked together for any purpose.

L.B.F. is a fellowship of Baptist pastors. There are many instances in the New Testament where pastors fellowshipped together to further the cause of Christ. Paul and Barnabas visited the elders at Jerusalem to solve a theological problem. Paul visited the churches of the Mediterranean world to take up an offering for the saints in Jerusalem. Paul encouraged one church to pray for another church. Paul was sent out by the Antioch church to establish New Testament churches in Cyprus and Asia Minor. In all these occasions there was a fellowship by men of God to carry out the purpose of the local church, which is the Great Commission.

The Liberty Baptist Fellowship is made up of men walking together on the same road, going in the same direction. Each church, is like soldiers in an army, listening to the cadence beat of its commander, but none are directed by his fellows. Under no circumstances does one church or pastor give orders to another, for all swear allegiance to the commander Jesus Christ. But like an army whose strength is in its mass, so Liberty Baptist Fellowship can plant 5,000 new churches before the year 2000 by doing together what cannot be done separately.

Liberty Baptist Fellowship will be controlled by a National Committee of twelve pastors who are elected to serve a three-year term of office. A president will be elected annually to chair the business meeting of the fellowship and supervise the business of the Fellowship. Since this is a Baptist Fellowship of Baptist pastors, the members of the National Committee will be elected by their peers.

Dr. Falwell will serve as National Chairman because he is pastor of Thomas Road Baptist Church and Chancellor of Liberty Baptist College. As a permanent officer, he will give stability to the organization. The National Chairman will direct the program at the national conventions.

Since this is a fellowship of pastors who lead their churches, the bills must be paid by them. If every church, no matter how small, will make a monthly offering the bills can be covered. Of all the missionary projects your church will support, this may have the greatest potential of multiplication, because you will be helping to plant churches.

> The Liberty-Type Church
>
> 1. Fundamentalist
> 2. Super-aggressive evangelism
> 3. Growth oriented
> 4. Biblical separation (personal and ecclesiastical)
> 5. Independent
> 6. Baptist

Release Immediately

Name
Address
City, State, Zip
Telephone

Begin typing half page down

       The _____(name of church)_____ will hold its first meeting in _____(location)_____, at ___(address)____ _____ on Sunday, ____(date)_____. Pastor _____(name)_____ has been in the area for __(length of time)__ gathering those who are interested in the new church. __(last name)__ is a graduate of 19(___) ____(name of college)_____ and 19(___) graduate of ____(name of Seminary)_____ receiving the ___(__)___ degree.

      __(last name)__ indicated the church will be an independent Baptist church with no denominational affiliation. He testified, "Our church is conservative in nature and our doctrinal statement is taken from the historic New Hampshire Conference of faith; which indicates we follow the traditional beliefs of Baptists." The pastor added, "We will be evangelistic in outreach because the purpose of the church is found in the Great Commission." The aggressive soul winning nature of the church is translated in numerical attendance goals. The pastor has told those who are interested in the new church that he has set a goal of 100 in attendance within the first year. He also plans to offer all the services of a church and purchase land for a building within the year.

      The new venture is partly underwritten by the Liberty Baptist Fellowship for Church Planting in Lynchburg, Virginia, which is the home mission outreach of Thomas Road Baptist Church where Dr. Jerry Falwell is pastor. In the past eight year 171 new churches have been planted by students from the college, Seminary, and Bible Institute of the Liberty schools that are connected with the church. _____(last name)_____ feels the success of other graduates from Liberty is as indicative that he will reach his goals.

Dr. Elmer Towns, Dean of Liberty Baptist Seminary said, "I feel the academic record of _____(name if student)_____ and his faithful church work while a student is an indication that he can go plant a church."

_____(last name)_____ indicated the new church will begin with _____(number)_____ Sunday School classes at _____(time)_____ and the morning worship starts at _____(time)_____. Nursery will be provided for young babies.

-30-

To Church Planter

Retype this press release and take (do not mail) to the church editor before Wednesday of the week you will begin your first service.

FOR FURTHER STUDY

Amberson, Talmadge R., Ed. *The Birth of Churches.* Nashville, Tennessee: Broadman Press, 1979.

Belew, Wendell. *Churches and How They Grow.* Nashville, Tennessee: Broadman Press, nd.

Benson, Donald. *How to Start a Daughter Church.* Quezo City, Philippines: Filkoba Press, 1972.

Chapman, Kenneth. *How to Plant, Pastor and Promote a Local Church.* Lynchburg, Virginia: James Family Christian Publishers, 1979.

Chapman, Ken. *The Successful New Church.* Alta Vista, Virginia: Alta Vista Press, 1981.

Currin, James H. *Starting New Missions and Churches.* Nashville: The Sunday School Board, 1971.

Greenway, Roger S., Ed. *Guidelines for Urban Church Planting.* Grand Rapids, Michigan: Baker Book House, 1976.

Helton, Max. "The Making of a New Church" Hammond, Indiana: Helton Publications, nd. (series of six cassette tapes).

Hodges, Melvin L. *A Guide to Church Planting.* Chicago: Moody Press, 1973.

Hodges, Melvin L. *Growing Young Churches.* Chicago: Moody Press, nd.

Jones, Ezra Earl. *Strategies for New Churches.* New York: Harper & Row, 1976.

Longenecker, Harold L. *Building Town and Country Churches.* Chicago: Moody Press, 1973.

MacNair, Donald J. *The Birth, Care, and Feeding of a Local Church.* Washington, D.C., Canon Press, 1973.

Mooneyham, Lamarr. "Starting a Church From Scratch." Hillsborough North Carolina: Lamarr Mooneyham Productions, 1981, (Two taped lectures.)

Mooneyham, Lamarr. "Specifics in Church Planting." Hillsborough, North Carolina: Lamarr Mooneyham Productions, 1981 (Two taped lectures.)

Perkins, Ernie. *Guidelines for the Pioneer Pastor.* Fairborn, Ohio: Encounter Publishing Company, 1971.

Redford, Jack. *Guide for Establishing New Churches and Missions*. Nashville, Tennessee: Home Mission Board/Southern Baptist Convention, nd.

Redford, Jack. *Planting New Churches*. Nashville, Tennessee: Broadman Press, 1978.

Rice, Grant. "Church Planting Pre-Planning." Rockvale, Tennessee: Grant G. Rice, nd.

Seibel, Roy W. *Shepherding New Flocks*. (Self-published mimeograph notes.)

Starr, Timothy. *Church Planting: Always in Season*. Toronto: Published by author, 1978.

Thomas, Roy. *Planting and Growing a Fundamental Church*. Nashville, Tennessee: Randall House Publications, 1979.

Towns, Elmer L. *Getting a Church Started in the Face of Insurmountable Obstacles with Limited Resources in Unlikely Circumstances*. Nashville: Impact Books, 1975.

Watermann, L. P. *New Church Manual*. Wheaton, Illinois: The Conservative Baptist Home Missions Society, nd.

DIRECTORY

Lamarr Mooneyham Productions
Division of Freedom Enterprises
Route 4, Box 227-F
Hillsborough, NC 27278

Liberty Baptist Fellowship for Church Planting
P.O. Box 368
Madison Heights, VA 24572

Lighthouse Fellowship for Church Planting
P.O. Box 110213
Nashville, TN 37211

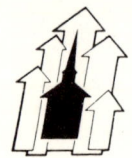

Church Growth Institute
Steps in Living Ministries, Inc.
P.O. Box 4404
Lynchburg, VA 24502